David Ruggerio's Italian Kitchen

David Ruggerio's
Italian

Artisan New York

Kitchen

Family Recipes from the Old Country

Photographs by Maura McEvoy

Also by David Ruggerio
Little Italy Cookbook

Published by Artisan
A Division of Workman Publishing, Inc.
708 Broadway
New York, New York 10003
www.workman.com

Library of Congress Cataloging-in-Publication Data
Ruggerio, David.
        David Ruggerio's Italian kitchen : family recipes from the old country /
    David Ruggerio ; photographs by Maura McEvoy.
            p.   cm.
        Includes index.
        ISBN 1-57965-115-1 (hardcover)
        1. Cookery, Italian—Southern style.   2. Cookery—
Italy—Naples.   3. Cookery—Italy—Sicily.   I. Title.
    TX723.2.S65R84   2000
    641.59457—dc21   98-50971
                                                        CIP

Printed at Arnoldo Mondadori Editore, Verona, Italy
10   9   8   7   6   5   4   3   2   1

Book design by Alexandra Maldonado

To my sons, Anthony and Paul, my reasons for living

Introduction viii

1 Antipasti Appetizers 1

2 Zuppe Soups 29

3 Pasta The Macaroni 49

4 Frutti di Marc Fish and Shellfish 89

5 Carne e Pollame Meat and Fowl 125

6 Verdure Vegetables 163

7 Dolci Desserts 187

Basic Recipes 216

Acknowledgments 222

Index 223

Contents

Italian Family Cuisine

When I was searching for a theme for my second book, I didn't have to look very far. In my first book, I explored the culinary delights of my upbringing in Little Italy. For the second, I decided I wanted to go back home—to my roots in Italy. Although I was born and bred in the good old U.S. of A., my family always maintained strong ties to the old country. Nowhere was it more evident than in the kitchen. My grandmother brought me up, and her kitchen was the hub around which family life revolved. She taught us all how to cook, how to eat, and she never ceased to remind us where her recipes came from—her mother (my great-grandmother) and her mother before her and so and so forth.

Sometimes, a culture tends to get lost as the younger generations assimilate into the American way of life. Not so in my family. The connection remained vital because not only did we stay in touch with relatives on the other side of the Atlantic, visiting them whenever possible, but we lived the Italian family life each and every day and we ate Italian every night. This book is my homage to the strength of our Italian family and to the cuisine that sustained it.

Naples and Sicily *Fire and Water*

I consider myself 100 percent pure, unadulterated Italian, but I have two separate and distinct strains running throught my veins: Sicilian and Neapolitan. From the perspective of most Americans, Italy is one country; an Italian is an Italian. A quick reference to the history books, however, reveals that a unified Italy is a pretty new concept, much newer than, say, the Thirteen Colonies or the United States of America. Although the geographical distances in Italy are shorter, Sicily is about as far culturally from northern Italy as New England is from the Arizona desert.

As I thought about this book, I kept bumping into the contrasts between the land of my mother, Naples, and that of my father, Sicily. Both areas are part of the beautiful patchwork that is Italy; both are important sources of great traditions and cooking. They were also the two main departure points of immigrants—overwhelmingly poor and southern—who helped build America. So now I, two or three generations after my brave ancestors left, hoping to find a better life in the New World, decided to go back to rediscover the richness and diversity of what they left behind.

My roots in Sicily and Naples were evident every day as I grew up, nowhere more powerfully than in the cuisine, which is such an important part of our Italian culture. This is a book of recipes that have come from Italy, either directly or indirectly. I've collected them on my visits back to the old country to meet and greet friends and relatives. Some of these people have given me their recipes out of the generosity of their hearts. In other cases, I've adapted my own versions of old standbys or created new ones based on what I've seen and tasted. Nothing beats a trip "home" to Italy, a land of endless culinary inspiration. Short of that, I can save the airfare, take a trip to the kitchen instead, put on some music, and "cook Italian." That takes me back, too.

I think of my dual heritage—Neapolitan and Sicilian—as two tremendous gifts, two different parts of my personality and of the personality of this book. They're like two opposites coming together, contrasting but compatible. They're two parts that make the whole greater than their sum.

Naples is the fire. It's got excitement, it's got heat. You see it, you know what you're getting. Naples is friendly, dynamic, in your face. It's on the surface. What it's got to offer is right there for the taking. Sicily, on the other hand, seems deeper, more brooding. If Naples jumps right out at you like fire, then Sicily runs silent and deep like the sea. Another way I like to put it is, Naples discovers you, but you discover Sicily.

As you'll see, I've divided each chapter of this book into two sections, one for Naples, one for Sicily. I've tried to achieve a balance between the two—in the number and types of recipes offered as well as through the photographs, recipe notes, and stories.

Naples *My Passion*

Growing up, I always considered Naples my home. What I mean to say is I grew up in a Neapolitan household. If I'm Sicilian by character, I'm Neapolitan by emotion. The Neapolitan side is where I get my passion for life and for cooking. In Naples, it's hard not to fall in love. Neapolitans are a fun-loving people—passionate about their music, their families, their culture, and especially their cooking. In that sense, my mother's family is typically Neapolitan.

When my family went to see people off or to pick them up at the steamship piers on the Hudson River in Manhattan, it was always the boat to or from Naples. When we went back to Italy, it was always to Naples first. We'd stay at the homes of friends or family or sometimes in a hotel. A trip to Italy usually involved visits to family up in the mountains, but it was much more fun to stay by the Bay of Naples. That's where the action was.

Naples, to me, was always much more lively and fun. Sicily, on the other hand, was more serious, more profound. I associate Naples with those happy-go-lucky days of childhood, while Sicily was something that grew on me—not kid stuff. Sure, Sicily is a beautiful place to visit. You can go sightseeing there just as you can all over Italy and be bowled over by the grandeur of its natural beauty—rocky coastlines plunging to aquamarine seas, the stark beauty of the rugged interior of the island, and so forth. You would be amazed by the layers upon layers of culture and history—for example, did you know that Sicily has some of the best Greek temples anywhere, including Greece itself? And yet it takes a lot longer to gain a true appreciation of Sicily. Once you spend time there, get to know the people, you begin to feel the depth of its culture. Palermo, on the surface, looks like any bustling city in Italy, except it's a little hotter and there are a few more palm trees. But after a while its Sicilian character starts to emerge.

The same differences show up in the cooking. Neapolitan cooking is very colorful, very accessible, the basic ingredients and combinations just jump right out at you. Sicilian cooking is not so colorful, but more complex, more subtle. It's got some "exotic" ingredients that add a little something more interesting or intriguing to the mix.

When I say we're from Naples, that's a bit of an oversimplification. For my mother's mother's family, home is actually Sant'Angelo dei Lombardi, a town about fifty miles to the east of Naples, beyond Avellino in the mountains of Irpinia. On my mother's father's side, they came from Avellino. It is important to recognize, though, that the Neapolitan culture and cuisine exert a strong influence far and wide.

My mother's family has had its share of tragedy, which is not unusual among our people. It started with my great-grandfather Allesandro, who was the result of a midnight rendezvous between the monsignor and a local seventeen-year-old girl. Upon his birth, he was placed in an orphanage in Avellino. Later, he was adopted by a family named Lazzarino. He grew up, got married, and eventually fathered eleven children, of whom my grandfather, Leonard, was the youngest. When my grandfather was very young, his father was murdered by his own stepbrother in an argument, leaving my great-grandmother Concetta to raise the children alone. Who would marry a widow with eleven kids? Somehow she managed with a perseverance and sense of humor that was famous among all the people she knew.

Typical of the women of Avellino, my great-grandmother was a terrific cook. She was economical with her ingredients, but extravagant when it came to the amount of food she prepared. (I guess this becomes second nature with so many kids.)

There is something about Neapolitan cooking that has made it representative of all Italian cooking in the minds of most Americans. Everybody in this country recognizes the basic ingredients: olive oil, garlic, tomatoes, pasta, seafood. . . . Did I forget Mario Lanza? Yes, it's true, my great-grandmother couldn't function without Mario Lanza. His golden voice filled up the background of her life; his singing was the catalyst for whatever she did—shopping, cooking and serving the meals, cleaning the house.

My first ancestor to come over was my great-grandfather Giuseppe Pesce, known as Andrea. We have the certificate of his arrival in New York, dated 1911, on the German steamer *Friedrich der Grosse*, North German Lloyd Steamship Co., which docked on April 3, 1907. Andrea was from Sant'Angelo and he married a hometown girl, Antoinette Claro (the Americanized version of Quagliariello). Antoinette was a tough lady who carried fifty-pound bags of lard from the pork store and once knocked a bus driver out cold with a roll of change because he insulted her. (My great-grandfather bought her a bicycle after that so she wouldn't have to take the bus to work anymore.)

Antoinette and Andrea had three kids: Pasquale ("Uncle Pat" or "Patsy"), Michael, and Mary, my grandmother, who raised me. My grandmother married Leonard Lazzarino, that young gentleman from Avellino who was the youngest of eleven kids. They all settled in Brooklyn, but they never lost their Neapolitan culture. I was trained in classical French cuisine here and in France, but will always return to my roots in Brooklyn and Italy. And I wish the same for my sons, Anthony and Paul—that they experience the world but always come home.

My mother, Constance, who passed away when I was young, was one of three children born to the Lazzarinos. She married Richard Ruggerio, my father, from the distant island of . . . you guessed it, Sicily.

Sicily *My Heart and Soul*

I have a love for Sicily that is hard to put into words. It is my heart and soul; it defines my character. Sicily is the Italy of fifty years ago, full of folklore and traditions. What I mean is that in so many ways Sicily hasn't been affected by "modern progress." Because of that she holds on to her old customs, some of them especially strict by our standards. Yes, there is a veneer of modernity in Sicily, but deep down it's the old traditions that define the culture.

My father comes from a small town in Sicily about forty miles west of Palermo called Castellammare del Golfo. Although it's a quiet modest place by Italian standards, its significance to the Italian-American community is way out of proportion to its size because so many industrious immigrants came from there to America and they, in turn, begot so many of the rest of us.

Sicily is an island apart from the rest of Italy. Some of the old aristocracy of Sicily still pray for secession from the mainland so they can claim their old titles and authority. There is nobility and tragedy, melancholy and poverty, in the people who struggle to eke out their existence in Sicily's rugged interior. With its parched wheat fields and barren rocky terrain, it has a desertlike quality in the summer. That's no wonder because if you keep going south, it's not far before you hit the sandy deserts of North Africa. The island of Pantelleria, off the southwest coast of Sicily, where they produce the big juicy capers sold in salt, is just fifty miles from Tunisia.

There's a popular misconception of Sicilians as a bunch of rough peasants dressed in black, stuck in the nineteenth century, and ruled by a few noblemen living in their luxurious villas and castles. That may have been true when my ancestors came to America. In fact, they were trying to escape that type of hard life in a feudalistic society. Nowadays, there are still many Sicilians living traditional lifestyles and struggling to make a living off the land. But there is also a huge urban population in Sicily's sophisticated cosmopolitan capital, Palermo (with over 700,000 residents), and in its other cities—people who would be equally at home in my native Brooklyn. These are the modern Sicilians. They've got one foot in the twenty-first century and the other in the nineteenth, keeping the old traditions alive.

The heritage of Sicily goes back to ancient Greek, Roman, and even prehistoric times. Sicilians are a proud and stubborn people. When I tell my American friends about some of the old customs they think I'm pulling their legs. "Is this stuff for real?" they ask. Absolutely! When a boy wants to date a Sicilian girl, for example, he's going to have to contend with her whole family—legions of relatives chaperoning their every move. A romantic night on the town, one-on-one? *Fuh-ged-aboud-it!* Some of those old clichés—a young man and woman strolling down the street together, thirty relatives of hers, most of them dressed in black, trailing a half a block behind—are still true to this day.

Sicily has been subjected to foreign rule on many occasions during its long history. Each of these conquerors has left behind a few of its customs and practices, including, of course, its cooking. Thus Sicily has been blessed with an unusual variety of produce and a cuisine that you wouldn't think of as traditionally Italian. If you look closely you will find traces of Greece, not just in the magnificent temples at Segesta and Agrigento, but all across the landscape. It was the Greeks who brought the olive, now thought of as a native tree. A sweet wine called Malvasia is still made today in the same way they made it in ancient Greece. Cheeses are still made as described by Homer in the *Odyssey*. Going back even further, Bacchus, the ancient god of wine and revelry, is said to have planted grapes at the foot of Mount Etna, Sicily's great volcano.

The native tribes of Sicily were the Siculi in the south and the Sicani in the west. The Arabs, known by the intriguing name of Saracens during the Crusades, ruled Sicily for three hundred years (A.D. the eighth through the tenth centuries), leaving behind one of Sicily's greatest assets—citrus. Today, Sicilian oranges and lemons are considered among the world's best. The Arabs also left behind rice and sugarcane. With an abundance of sugar, Sicily developed a sweet tooth, which I share and which is reflected today in an extraordinary array of sweets. (See Chapter 7 for dessert recipes.)

The Saracens were conquered by the Normans, who in turn yielded to the Spaniards (Aragons, to be exact). They left behind peppers, squash, beans, and tomatoes. It is impossible to think of Sicilian cooking without these ingredients.

There are also many fabulous ingredients native to Sicily, such as the saffron that grows wild in the Madonie Mountains. It's just one of the many ancient, fragrant, and exotic flavors of Sicilian cuisine. Lavender also grows wild all over the island. Typically, the women in my family pride themselves on their handmade linens. My grandmother has some that were made by relatives a hundred years ago. And in the linen closets, you'll always find sachets of dried lavender, lending the most wonderful natural perfume to those precious heirloom cloths.

I've always been amazed that fragrant plants and herbs grow wild in the countryside in places like Sicily. It's a treat for a city boy like me, particularly one whose profession relies on his sense of smell and taste, to go out and breathe in lungsful of fresh air teeming with herbal aromas. Wild mountain fennel is another of these naturally occurring herbs, and of course the Sicilians have found numerous clever ways of working it into the cuisine.

*   *   *

This book is about the connection between me and my people and our ancestral homeland—Italy. Sometimes we have nothing more than a trinket, an old faded photograph, or a piece of paper like that certificate of arrival concerning my great-grandfather. The people are long gone, the possibility of visiting the homeland is sometimes no more than a dream. No matter, because we keep that connection alive in our memories—and in our kitchens—and we keep our memories fresh by celebrating our culture. What better way to celebrate our culture than through its wonderful cuisine? So read on and enjoy while I share with you some of my favorite recipes from the old country.

—David Ruggerio

New York City

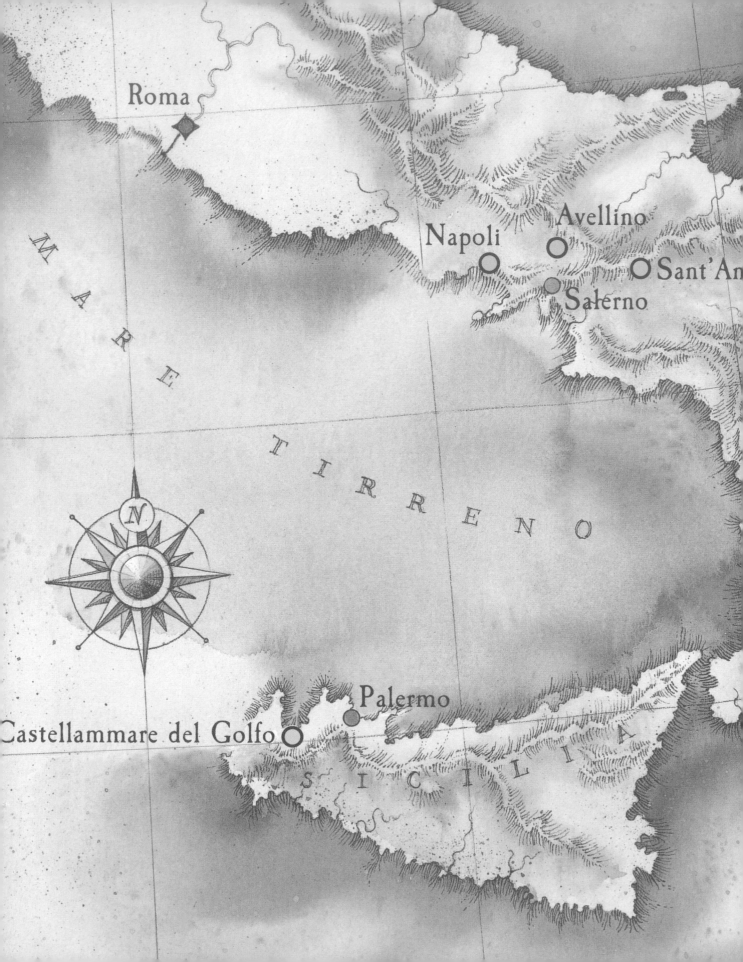

antipasti

*My great-grandmother
and -grandfather Antoinette
and Andrea Pesce*

Italians love their multicourse meals, starting with the appetizer course, followed by pasta, entrée, side dishes, possibly a salad, fruits and/or desserts with coffee. Now, that would seem like an excessive amount of food, but the Italians pull it off. How? They don't overeat.

If you want to create a really special feast, put together an *antipasto misto*, an assortment of five to ten appetizers. With a little resourcefulness and planning—and some simple-to-prepare recipes like the ones in this chapter—you can really wow your guests.

Just about every restaurant on the Italian peninsula offers an *antipasto misto*, with all kinds of regional variations and chefs' signature dishes. Although Neapolitans and Sicilians approach *antipasti* in similar ways, a difference emerges in the ingredients. The first thing you notice in Sicily is the influence of other Mediterranean cuisines, particularly those of North Africa and Greece. With *antipasti*, the chef has more of a chance to be creative, which is why foreign influences are so common. *Antipasti* can be the opener for a multicourse feast or, in and of themselves, they can be a buffet meal for a cocktail party.

Cavolo Ripieno

Stuffed Savoy Cabbage with Pork and Pine Nuts

Italians are honest, hardworking people. When it comes to making money, they have a largely undeserved reputation for creativity and scheming. Like many large families, however, my family had one relative for whom we always had to make excuses. That was my Uncle Tony. I remember when we were kids, we would occasionally take long car rides to visit him. When he went away, we'd always ask my aunt where he was, and she would answer in her best broken English, "He's in-a college!" Uncle Tony was away at "college" for an awfully long time. There were always delicious care packages sent to him there, and this recipe was one of them.

Note: Savoy cabbage is the most delicately flavored of its genre, which is why chefs prefer it for cooking. Always look for cabbages that feel heavy for their size and have healthy-looking outside leaves.

Pancetta is Italian-style bacon, cured but not smoked. If you can't find it, regular bacon is an acceptable substitute.

1 head savoy cabbage

¼ cup finely diced pancetta

1 medium white onion, peeled and finely chopped

½ cup pine nuts, lightly toasted in the oven and roughly chopped

½ pound ground pork

1 tablespoon chopped fresh Italian parsley

1 teaspoon chopped fresh sage

1 cup Chicken Stock (page 216)

½ cup freshly grated Parmesan cheese

Preheat the oven to 375°F.

Carefully peel off the large outer leaves of the cabbage. (You should have about 16 leaves, each 6 to 8 inches wide.) Blanch them in a large pot of boiling salted water until they are pliable, about 2 minutes. Refresh the leaves under cold water, then set aside to drain. Be careful not to overcook the leaves, i.e., until they're totally limp.

Cut out and discard the core from the rest of the cabbage, then chop it into medium dice. Sauté the pancetta in a skillet, over medium heat for 2 to 3 minutes, then add the onion and chopped cabbage and cook for 5 more minutes. Remove these ingredients to a bowl, then stir in the pine nuts and chopped herbs. Sauté the pork in the same skillet until lightly browned, 3 to 4 minutes. Drain excess fat from the pork, add it to the bowl, and mix all the ingredients well.

Place the blanched cabbage leaves on a flat surface, and spoon about 1½ tablespoons of the stuffing into the center of each of the 16 leaves. Roll up the leaves and place them side by side, almost touching, in a greased baking pan. Pour the chicken stock over the rolls, sprinkle them with Parmesan, and bake for 25 minutes or until the cheese is browned. Serve immediately.

Serves 8

Crostata di Carciofi e Funghi

Artichoke and Mushroom Tart

Artichokes and mushrooms—both have different earthy, delicious flavors in and of themselves. They also happen to make a great combination. Here is a recipe that takes advantage of that combo. One great thing about these types of tarts is that they're equally good served hot or cold, as a snack, lunch, or appetizer.

For the dough

2¼ cups presifted all-purpose flour

10 tablespoons unsalted butter, at room temperature

Pinch of salt

⅓ cup ice water

For the filling

4 medium artichokes

3½ tablespoons extra-virgin olive oil

Salt and freshly ground black pepper to taste

2 tablespoons dry white wine

2 tablespoons Chicken Stock (page 216) or water

1 tablespoon unsalted butter

½ pound white mushrooms, cleaned and sliced

2 ounces pancetta, cut into ¼-inch dice

2 large eggs

½ cup heavy cream

½ cup milk

3½ ounces shredded caciocavallo cheese (mozzarella is an acceptable substitute)

TO PREPARE THE DOUGH: Combine the flour, butter, salt, and water in a bowl. Mix lightly until the dough just comes together—don't overmix. Wrap in plastic and set aside in the refrigerator for at least 30 minutes.

TO PREPARE THE FILLING: Pull off and discard the tough outer leaves of the artichokes. Slice them in half lengthwise and scoop out the fuzzy chokes from the center. Cut the artichokes lengthwise into ¼-inch-thick slices.

Heat 2 tablespoons of the olive oil in a skillet over medium-high heat. Sauté the artichoke slices, lightly browning on both sides. Season the slices lightly with salt and pepper, then add the white wine and chicken stock. Cook till the liquid has evaporated. Remove the artichoke slices from the pan and reserve.

Place the butter and remaining olive oil in the skillet, add the mushrooms and sauté over high heat. Lightly season with salt and pepper. When they are lightly browned, remove the mushrooms from the pan and reserve. Add the pancetta and cook until lightly browned, then drain the fat and reserve. Place the eggs, cream, milk, and salt and pepper to taste in a bowl and beat until well combined.

Preheat the oven to 425°F.

Roll out the dough into a 16- to 18-inch round, ⅛ inch thick. Lightly butter a 9-inch springform pan, then line it with the dough. Trim any excess dough that overhangs the edges of the pan and discard. Fill the pan with the artichokes, mushrooms, pancetta, and caciocavallo cheese, then pour in the egg-cream mixture to complete the filling. Bake for 30 minutes or until the mixture is set and the pastry is golden brown.

Serves 8

Foglie di Basilico Ripiene

Basil "Sandwiches"

These little fried delights actually use pieces of mozzarella as the "bread" for the "sandwiches." You can grow basil like a weed in your own garden, and there's nothing quite like picking those big, fragrant leaves in midsummer and using them right away in your favorite recipes.

Olive oil, particularly the rich, green high-quality extra-virgin type, is often inappropriately heavy for frying. It also imposes its own flavor on a food. In Italy, when they want to fry seafood or other dishes to a tempuralike lightness, they use a lighter vegetable oil, usually sunflower oil. In the States, we usually turn to canola oil, which is light and neutral-tasting, an excellent choice for deep-frying.

1 cup all-purpose flour

Salt and freshly ground black pepper

2 tablespoons extra-virgin olive oil

1 extra-large egg, white and yolk separated

3 tablespoons dry white wine

½ cup cold water

One 8-ounce piece fresh mozzarella cheese, cut into ½-inch-thick slices

30 fresh basil leaves

Canola or other light vegetable oil for frying

Sift the flour into a bowl with a pinch of salt and pepper. Stir in the olive oil, egg yolk, white wine, and cold water with a wooden spoon, mix well, then allow to stand covered at room temperature for 2 hours.

Pat the mozzarella slices dry and cut them into 1-inch squares. Make miniature three-layer sandwiches with 2 basil leaves between 3 squares of mozzarella. Skewer each one with a toothpick to hold it together.

Beat the egg white until it forms stiff peaks, then fold it into the batter. Place the oil in a heavy-bottomed pot to a depth of 3 inches and preheat over a medium-high flame. Test the oil by dropping a small amount of batter in; if it floats and sizzles right away, the oil is hot enough to begin frying. Dip the sandwiches in the batter and deep-fry until golden brown on all sides. Remove, pat dry on paper towels, slide the toothpicks out, sprinkle lightly with salt, and serve hot.

Serves 6

Mozzarella di Bufala

You've heard of buffalo mozzarella? Well, that's the Americanized name for *mozzarella di bufala*, which is the variety that sets the standard for all mozzarella. Although it can also be made from cow's milk, the best mozzarella is made from the milk of water buffalo and it comes from one of two main production zones in Italy, both in Campania: on the coastal plain south of Salerno or in the area around Caserta, just north of Naples.

If you continue south from the city of Naples, down past the Amalfi coast and the busy port city of Salerno, after about sixty miles you come to Paestum, which has some of the most famous Greek temples in all of the Mediterranean. Practically within the shadow of these temples, in the surrounding community of Capaccio, is where you find the *bufala*, the beautiful horned cows that are responsible for genuine fresh mozzarella.

Compared to the milk from your everyday cow, the milk from the horned cow is creamier and richer, and it makes a cheese that has a nuttier flavor. Legend has it that the Norman kings brought the bufala from Sicily, where they were first introduced by the Arabs in the eleventh century. Other experts claim they've been raised on the peninsula since late Greek or early Roman times. The bufala are big, slow, strong animals, like oxen, that like to cool off on a hot summer's day by wallowing in cool water, dirt, and mud.

The other center for buffalo mozzarella production is in Caserta, just about fifteen miles north of Naples. In the mid-1700s the Bourbon king of Naples wanted to be just like Louis XIV of France so he built his own version of Versailles, the huge palace and gardens outside Paris. He chose Caserta as the site for his extravagance, right in the middle of a fertile plain where the bufala graze and the mozzarella is made. Most people have long since forgotten the king and his palace, but the mozzarella lives on.

Mozzarella is the most famous member of the family of *pasta filata* cheeses, which includes provolone, caciocavallo, and scamorza. *Filata* means stretched, pulled, or spun, as in spinning yarn, and that's what they do to the curd to create the cheeses.

The key to mozzarella, which is sometimes referred to as *fior di latte* ("flower of milk"), is that it has to be fresh. Any authentic producer makes a new batch every day, assuring that it reaches the consumer as quickly as possible, under refrigerated conditions. Factory or machine-made mozzarella doesn't have the butterfat that the real handmade version has, and it shows. It's just not as rich and creamy. The texture is harder and more uniform, almost rubbery, and the flavor is bland.

To make mozzarella, they start with big blocks of milk curd. First they cut it up and then pass it through a *chitarra*, a bigger version of the slotted or wired device that they use to create *maccheroni alla chitarra*, a type of pasta cut from sheets. Next, the cut-up curds are subjected to a very hot bath where they recoagulate. After that, the cheesemaker works his art and magic, waiting till just the right moment to begin the "pulling" process, which consists of kneading the curds into a smooth mass using a wooden paddle. Then handfuls of the curd are pulled off. *Mozzare* is the verb, meaning "to chop off" or "lop off," and that's where the cheese gets its name. After the curds are shaped into the familiar balls, they take another bath in ice water, which ends the "cooking" action of the hot water.

Some mozzarella is salted, in which case it's given a preliminary bath in brine. Mozzarella can also be smoked, resulting in *mozzarella affumicata*, which is a really delicious variation.

The standard size for Italian mozzarella is a roughly spherical shape weighing 250 grams, or a little over half a pound. It also comes in *ciliegine* ("little cherries"), tiny 15-gram (half-ounce) balls, as well as *bocconcini* ("little mouthfuls") of 50 grams, or 2 ounces, about one inch in diameter. Sometimes it comes in braids, which can be as big as 3 kilos, or 6½ pounds.

One of my favorite dishes is a summer platter of fresh mozzarella di bufala slices alternating with tomato and basil picked right out of the garden, drizzled with a little extra-virgin olive oil.

Insalata di Tonno e Fagioli

Tuna and White Bean Salad

Here is an excellent rendition of an appetizer salad that you'll encounter all around the Naples area. This recipe calls for canned tuna, but if you have fresh tuna by all means use it. It also reminds me of one of my pet peeves. I've noticed that in preparing a meal, people will search out the best wine, the best olive oil, the best produce, and then settle for some lousy vinegar they found on sale for a few dollars less. As all chefs know, any dish is only as good as its ingredients. Do yourself a favor and don't skimp on anything—even the vinegar.

1 cup dried white navy beans, soaked overnight in the refrigerator with enough water to cover, then cooked until tender

2 tablespoons capers, rinsed

1 small red onion, peeled, thinly sliced, and soaked in cold water for 1 hour

Salt and freshly ground black pepper to taste

One 7-ounce can tuna, packed in oil, drained

⅓ cup extra-virgin olive oil

2 tablespoons red wine vinegar (or more to taste)

1 head radicchio, broken into individual leaves

Place the cooked white beans in a bowl with the capers and onion, and season with salt and pepper. Add the tuna, breaking it into large flakes, then the oil and vinegar. Toss well. Arrange the radicchio leaves around the perimeter of your platter, spoon the salad into the center, and serve.

Serves 4

Padellata di Porcini

Braised Porcini Mushrooms

Porcini have been a favorite of the Italians since ancient Roman times when cautious senators would prepare mushroom stews with their own hands for fear of the addition of "ambiguous toadstools" either by accident or design. Today gathering the porcini in early fall is an Italian national pastime. They can be fried, grilled, or braised and are incredibly delicious any way you make them.

3 tablespoons extra-virgin olive oil

3 cloves garlic, peeled and crushed

1½ pounds fresh porcini mushrooms, lightly brushed to remove any dirt (see Note)

2 ripe plum tomatoes, peeled, seeded, and coarsely chopped

½ cup dry white wine

Salt and freshly ground black pepper to taste

1 tablespoon chopped fresh mint

1 tablespoon chopped fresh Italian parsley

Heat the olive oil in a large skillet over medium-high heat. Add the garlic and porcini and cook for 2 minutes, stirring occasionally. Add the tomatoes and cook for another 2 minutes. Deglaze with the wine, lightly season with salt and pepper, and cook for 5 minutes more. Sprinkle with the herbs, toss, and serve.

Serves 4

Note: If you can't find fresh porcini for this recipe, you can substitute portobello or large shiitake; the dish will taste different but nevertheless delicious.

Pagnotelle Farcite

Savory Stuffed Buns

Even in Italy, these delicious little buns are not widely known. That's because they're so good the Neapolitans want to keep them a secret. When you try them, you'll understand what I mean and you'll want to give me a big kiss for revealing this recipe.

For the dough

½ cup warm milk

1 tablespoon plus 1 teaspoon active dry yeast

3 tablespoons granulated sugar

1 cup plus ¾ cup all-purpose flour

1 large egg

2 tablespoons unsalted butter

Pinch of salt

For the filling

4 tablespoons unsalted butter, softened

1 clove garlic, peeled and chopped

½ pound fresh lump crabmeat, picked clean of any shells

1 tablespoon chopped tomato

Salt and freshly ground black pepper to taste

1 tablespoon chopped fresh basil

1 tablespoon chopped fresh Italian parsley

2 shallots, peeled and chopped

1 large egg, lightly beaten

Preheat the oven to 375°F.

TO PREPARE THE DOUGH: Combine 2 tablespoons of the milk, the yeast, 2 tablespoons of the sugar, and 2 tablespoons of the flour in a large mixing bowl. Mix well and set aside for 30 minutes. In another bowl, combine the egg, butter, salt, and the remaining milk, sugar, and flour. Using a wooden spoon or an electric mixer with the dough hook attached, mix these ingredients together until smooth and elastic, then combine with the mixture in the other bowl. Do not overmix. Cover and let rise for 1 hour at room temperature (72° to 80°F.).

TO PREPARE THE FILLING: Place 1 teaspoon of the butter in a skillet over medium heat. Sauté the garlic, crab, tomato, and salt and pepper for 2 minutes. Remove from the heat and allow to cool. Pour off any excess liquid, then mix well in a bowl with the remaining butter, herbs, shallots, and more salt and pepper to taste.

Punch the dough down and divide it into 12 equal portions, forming them into round balls. On a lightly floured surface, roll each ball out into a 6-inch circle.

Divide the filling into 12 equal portions, placing one portion onto each circle of dough. Take up and pinch together the edges of each dough circle and roll it into a ball, sealing in the filling. Place on a buttered baking pan, cover with a damp towel, and allow to rise for 25 minutes. Lightly brush with the beaten egg, then bake in the oven for 20 minutes or until golden brown. Serve immediately.

Serves 6

Schiacciata con Uve

Schiacciata with Grapes

I love this recipe because it is not only delicious, but unusual and rustic. Despite the fact that it includes grapes, it is not particularly sweet, so it easily qualifies as an antipasto. Although the recipe calls for the Red Ruby variety of grapes, you can substitute Flame seedless or any other type of red table grape.

The word *schiacciata* is a beautiful mouthful of Italian that means "crushed" or "totally flattened." It's hard to pronounce but it goes something like this (be sure to say it fast): "skee-ah-*cha*-tah."

I know you'll want to make this, but plan ahead, because this recipe calls for two 1-hour resting periods — first for the sponge and then for the dough to rise.

For the sponge
1 cup plus 1 tablespoon all-purpose flour
2 packages active dry yeast
¾ cup warm water

2½ pounds seedless Red Ruby grapes
¾ cup granulated sugar
½ teaspoon fennel seeds

For the dough
2½ cups all-purpose flour
2 tablespoons extra-virgin olive oil
Pinch of salt
½ cup warm water

TO PREPARE THE SPONGE: Place 1 cup of the flour in a bowl and make a well in the center. Dissolve the yeast in the water and pour the mixture into the well, incorporating all the ingredients together. Dust the top with the remaining flour, cover, and allow to rest in a warm place about 1 hour until it doubles in size.

Clean the grapes well, removing any stems. Place them in a bowl, add the sugar and fennel seeds, mix well, and reserve.

TO PREPARE THE DOUGH: Mound the flour and make a well in the center. Pour the sponge, olive oil, salt, and water into the well and incorporate all the ingredients together, mixing well. (This can be done either by hand or with an electric mixer.) Knead the dough on a lightly floured surface for 3 minutes.

Oil a 14-inch pizza pan. Divide the dough into 2 equal-sized spheres, then roll each piece out to a round that is ¼ inch thick and 16 inches in diameter. Lay 1 round on the pizza pan, distributing half the grapes on top of it. Cover with the remaining dough round, seal the edges, and top with the remaining grapes. Cover the pan and place in a warm place for 1 hour, allowing the dough to double in size.

Preheat the oven to 375°F.

Place the schiacciata in the oven and allow to bake for 1 hour. Remove from the oven and allow it to cool. Cut it into wedge-shaped pieces like a pizza and serve.

Serves 10

Porcini

Once you've tried good, fresh, properly prepared porcini, you'll be permanently hooked. From a culinary viewpoint, they are probably the most prized mushroom after truffles. They come from the *boletus edulis* family of wild mushrooms and have a delicious, very pronounced "woodsy" aroma and flavor, subtle yet distinct, with a smooth, rich consistency. Porcini are one of those foods that are so tasty, they're best utilized in a simple presentation that accentuates their essential flavors. They can be served on their own, grilled or sautéed with a little garlic and olive oil, then sprinkled with parsley. They work as an appetizer, a side dish, even as a main course in a vegetarian menu. They make a fantastic sauce for pasta as well as for chicken, meat, and even mild-flavored fish.

Fresh porcini can be found growing wild in the northwestern United States—Oregon and Washington State—but they don't have quite the same rich, nutty flavor as the ones from Italy or France, where they're called *cèpes*. In this country, you can buy fresh imported porcini in many specialty stores in season (fall and late spring), but they're expensive. If you find some nice firm, fresh ones, try slicing them superthin or shaving them directly onto a salad with a grater as they do in Italy. (This is also what is done with truffles.)

Dried porcini can be substituted for fresh in certain recipes, such as for pasta sauces and soups, but they don't work for braising, grilling, or in salads. They must be soaked in warm water to be reconstituted, then diced. Be sure to save the soaking water because it has tremendous flavor. Simply strain it and add it to the sauce or soup when you need a thinner.

Pizza del Lattaio

Potato Pizza

If you feel the way I do about potatoes, you are definitely going to fall in love with this recipe. One tip: Save the water used to boil the potatoes, cool it, and use it to make the dough, which will come out even more delicate and delicious. This pizza can be served hot or at room temperature, as a first course or appetizer, cut into small wedges and passed around as an hors d'oeuvre, or retrieved from the pantry as a midnight snack. Any way you do it, it's equally delectable.

Lattaio in Italian is "milkman," which in this case, I suppose, refers to the fact that there's lots of dairy (three types of cheese) in the recipe. The Asiago and fontina are two lovely semi-hard, fairly mild cheeses from the north, near the Alps. Asiago comes aged anywhere from two to nine months or more; like the pecorino cheeses, it becomes harder, sharper-tasting, and more suitable for grating as it ages. This recipe also features a potato dough, which, along with the three cheeses, gives it a really subtle and irresistible flavor medley.

1½ pounds baking potatoes, peeled

1 teaspoon active dry yeast

⅓ cup extra-virgin olive oil

½ teaspoon salt

4 cups all-purpose flour

3 ounces Asiago cheese, cut into ¼-inch cubes

3 ounces fontina cheese, cut into ¼-inch cubes

Freshly ground black pepper

1 sprig fresh rosemary, leaves only

2 ounces freshly grated Parmesan cheese

Preheat the oven to 425°F.

Cook the potatoes in lightly salted boiling water until they are easily pierced with a knife. Drain them, mash a quarter of them into a bowl, cut the remainder into small cubes, and reserve.

To make the dough, dissolve the yeast in 1 cup of warm water. Combine with ¼ cup of the olive oil, salt, and the mashed potatoes. Stir in the flour a little at a time, adding just enough to make a dough that does not stick to the sides of the bowl. Place the dough on a lightly floured surface and knead for 4 to 5 minutes until it reaches a smooth consistency. (This can also be achieved in an electric mixer with the dough hook.) Place the dough in a lightly oiled bowl. Cover the bowl with a wet towel or plastic wrap and let it rest in a warm place until the dough doubles in size, about 45 minutes.

Roll the dough out into a large circle ⅛ inch thick and about 15 inches in diameter. Place the dough on a pizza stone or baking sheet, sprinkle with the Asiago and fontina, and top with the cubed potatoes. Drizzle the remaining olive oil on top of the pizza, then sprinkle it with fresh pepper, rosemary, and Parmesan. Cover again with plastic wrap and allow to rise in a warm place for 25 minutes. Remove the plastic wrap, place in the oven, and bake for 35 minutes or until the crust is golden brown and crispy.

Serves 8

Arancini

Sicilian Rice Balls

As kids, my friends and I loved rice balls so much that we would even resort to a little deception when we didn't have enough money to pay for them. One of our best tricks was to pool all our money until it was at least twenty dollars. We'd get a twenty-dollar bill and write a telephone number on it. Then one of us would go into a neighborhood store and buy all the candy we could eat. The important thing was that the store had to be busy, lots of customers and commotion. We'd stash the candy, then someone would go into the store and buy one piece of gum with a dollar bill. After he got the change from the single, he'd look it over and exclaim that the cashier had made a mistake: "I gave you a twenty-dollar bill. In fact, I can prove it because I wrote my friend's phone number on it." Then he'd recite the phone number and collect the extra change. Mind you, this is not to say we were bad kids, just that we would try almost any scheme to obtain rice balls. They were that good.

Arancini, by the way, means "little oranges" in Italian; in this case, it refers to the size of the rice balls.

1 quart Chicken Stock (page 216)

½ teaspoon saffron threads, finely chopped

**Salt and freshly ground black pepper
   to taste**

2 cups Arborio rice (see Note, page 18)

1¾ cups Marinara Sauce (page 217)

**½ cup freshly grated pecorino romano
   cheese**

2 tablespoons extra-virgin olive oil

8 ounces pork, cut into small dice

1 medium onion, peeled and chopped

½ cup peas, fresh or frozen

4 large eggs

1½ cups fresh bread crumbs

Canola or other light vegetable oil for frying

Place the stock, saffron, and salt and pepper to taste in a saucepan over medium heat, and bring to a boil. Add the rice all at once and, stirring, allow it to come back to a boil. Cover, lower the heat, and allow to simmer for about 16 minutes or until the rice is cooked and dry. If you find the rice is cooked but still contains liquid, uncover it and continue cooking until it dries out. Remove the rice from the heat, add ¾ cup of the marinara sauce and the cheese, stirring well and allowing it to cool for at least 2 hours.

Place the olive oil in a skillet over medium heat. Add the pork, browning the meat evenly, then add the onion and cook for 3 minutes or until translucent and lightly browned. Add the remaining marinara sauce and allow to simmer over a low heat for about 45 minutes. Add the peas and cook for 3 more minutes. Remove the pan from the heat and allow to cool. Remove the meat from the pan with a slotted spoon, shred it with a fork, and add it back to the pan.

Add 2 of the eggs to the cooled rice mixture and combine well. Divide the mixture into 12 equal portions, flattening each portion into a pancake in the palm of your hand. Place 2 tablespoons of the meat mixture in the center of each pancake, gently closing it and then forming it into a ball. Place the finished balls on a cookie sheet.

(The recipe can be prepared up to this point in advance and the balls frozen until ready to be cooked. They will keep up to 1 month

frozen. To defrost, put them in the refrigerator a day in advance.)

Beat the remaining 2 eggs in a bowl. Spread the bread crumbs out on a separate plate. Roll each rice ball in the egg first, then the bread crumbs. Place the canola oil in a pot over medium-high heat to a depth of 2 inches. Fry a few balls at a time, browning them evenly on all sides. Do not overcrowd them. Drain the balls on paper towels and serve hot.

Makes 12 rice balls

Note: Arborio is the special type of Italian rice used to make risottos. The grains are shorter and fatter and they contain more starch, which makes them ideal for attaining that perfect risotto consistency—no longer soupy but not quite mealy.

Cacuocciuli sott'Olio

Artichokes Preserved in Olive Oil

Here is one of the tastiest artichoke recipes you'll ever come across, a staple of the Sicilian antipasto spread. These delectable morsels can be used in salads, to stuff focaccia, sliced for sandwiches, or just eaten alone, speared with a toothpick, for appetizers.

The artichoke was brought to Sicily by the Arabs in the 1400s by way of the silk trade between the Sicilians and the Nasrids. It quickly became a favorite. In fact, legend has it that Catherine de Médicis almost died from eating too many of them during a wedding party in 1575. *Madonn'!*

Special equipment: A 16-ounce jar, which should hold all the artichokes. Be aware that once trimmed, they are much smaller and also that they should be packed fairly tightly into the jar.

1 pound small artichokes (approximately 1 dozen, no more than 3 inches in diameter)

Juice of 2 lemons

4 cups dry white wine

2 cups white wine vinegar

Peel of 1 lemon

3 whole cloves

2 bay leaves

1½ teaspoons salt

8 whole black peppercorns

For the jar

2 whole cloves

1 bay leaf

4 whole black peppercorns

Extra-virgin olive oil as needed

Clean the artichokes and trim off the hard outer leaves, leaving only the tender inner ones. Cut the points off the inner leaves. Place the artichokes in a bowl of cold water with the lemon juice.

Place the wine, vinegar, lemon peel, cloves, bay leaves, salt, and peppercorns in a nonaluminum saucepan. Bring the mixture to a boil, drain the artichokes, and then add them to the saucepan, allowing them to simmer for 12 minutes or until tender. Drain the artichokes, and allow them to cool.

TO PREPARE THE JAR: Place the artichokes in a jar, add the cloves, bay leaf, peppercorns, and enough olive oil to cover by ½ inch. Don't seal the jar right away. Allow the artichokes time to settle and any pockets of air to come to the surface.

Serves 6

Note: The artichokes can be stored in the fridge for 2 to 3 weeks.

Fegato a Sette Cannoli

Sweet-and-Sour Pumpkin

Now, if you speak Italian, this is not a recipe for liver, and if you don't speak Italian, yes, *fegato* does mean liver. Allow me to explain. Many moons ago, near the Garraffello Fountain in the center of old Palermo, there was a guy who sold vegetables to the poor. He created this very famous dish, which everyone agreed tasted just like meat. So they called it *fegato.* Now this fountain had seven water spouts called *cannoli,*

which is where the *sette cannoli* comes from. Leave it to the Sicilians! One more thing: If you can't find pumpkin, you can use butternut or acorn squash.

2½ pounds pumpkin, peeled, seeded, and cut into ¼-inch-thick wedges

Coarse salt

Pure olive oil for frying

1 medium onion, peeled and thinly sliced

1½ teaspoons granulated sugar

5½ tablespoons white wine vinegar

¾ teaspoon salt

½ teaspoon freshly ground black pepper

6 sprigs fresh mint, coarsely chopped

Lightly sprinkle the pumpkin wedges with salt. Place olive oil to a depth of ¼ inch in a large skillet over medium-high heat. Gently fry the pumpkin wedges until golden on both sides, about 5 minutes. Do not overcrowd the skillet as you fry. Drain the pumpkin on paper towels.

Lower the heat to medium, drain all but 3 tablespoons of the oil from the skillet, add the onion, sprinkle the sugar on, and sauté for about 15 minutes or until golden brown. Add the vinegar and ¼ cup of water. Cook until the liquid is reduced by half, stirring constantly. Arrange the wedges of pumpkin on a plate, spooning the liquid over the top; sprinkle with salt and pepper, then the mint. Allow to cool, and serve at room temperature.

Serves 6

Focaccia cu Brocculi Rabi

Focaccia Stuffed with Broccoli Rabe

It never ceases to amaze me how many people are opting for vegetarian choices. I'm not talking about radical vegetarians, but average people who are simply becoming more health conscious. Which means they're eating more greens, of which broccoli rabe is a stellar example.

You can have a lot of fun creating variations on this recipe, for example, by substituting other types of greens for the broccoli rabe or adding complementary ingredients such as roasted peppers, fresh basil, or even eggplant. To make the preparation easier, you can make the focaccia ahead, filling it the day you plan to serve it. Focaccia can be stored in the fridge, wrapped in plastic; it also freezes very well.

2 large bunches broccoli rabe, washed and trimmed of any tough stems

¼ cup extra-virgin olive oil

3 cloves garlic, peeled and chopped

¼ teaspoon crushed red pepper flakes

Salt and freshly ground black pepper

½ recipe Focaccia (page 220)

2 cups freshly grated mozzarella cheese

¼ cup freshly grated Parmesan cheese

Preheat the oven to 300°F.

Blanch the broccoli rabe in boiling salted water for 4 minutes to reduce any bitterness. Drain well and chop coarsely.

Place the olive oil in a large skillet over medium-high heat and sauté the garlic for 2 minutes or until golden brown. Add the red pepper flakes and the chopped broccoli. Sauté for 5 minutes, season with salt and pepper to taste, and reserve.

Slice the focaccia in half lengthwise, sprinkling the bottom half with half the mozzarella and Parmesan. Place the broccoli rabe on top of the cheese, sprinkle the remaining cheese on top of the broccoli rabe, cover with the top half of the focaccia, and bake in the oven for about 12 minutes or until the cheese is well melted. Cut into wedges and serve.

Serves 4

Insalata di Mulinciani alla Pina

Pina's Eggplant Salad

Eggplant to Italians is like sex to nymphomaniacs. They can't live without it. The question often arises: how to pick the best eggplants? First, everyone agrees that they must be firm and feel heavy for their size. After that the argument begins as to which ones have the least seeds, the most bitterness, and so forth. Some people say they must be light purple in color, some say ivory or even striped!

Pina is an old friend of our family and a wonderful cook who lives in a small village outside Palermo. She not only makes this excellent salad, but claims to know the definitive standard for selecting eggplants, which is to look for ones with a dimple on the bottom; they're the females and they have far fewer seeds.

And don't forget to select a good vinegar. Use the same standards as you would for buying wine. Cheap vinegar does nothing for your salads or marinades. There is a time to be cheap. Buying vinegar is not one of them. Look for a good imported vinegar; it will make all the difference.

Peel the eggplants, cut them in half lengthwise, then cut them into ½-inch half-moon-shaped slices. Poach them for 8 minutes in a large pot of lightly salted boiling water. Remove them from the pot and refresh under cold water. Drain the slices thoroughly, squeezing them gently, then patting them dry with a paper towel. Blanch the onion slices for 1 minute in the same pot of boiling water.

On a large platter, alternate slices of eggplant and strips of peppers until you fill the platter. Sprinkle the onion slices over all. Combine the mint, garlic, lemon zest, and salt and pepper in a mixing bowl. Whisk in the olive oil and vinegar. Spoon the dressing over the salad and allow to stand for 1 hour before serving. Serve at room temperature.

Serves 8

Note: This salad can be stored, covered, in the fridge for a few days, but be sure to allow it to come back up to room temperature before serving. It's just not good to serve it cold.

2 eggplants, about 1½ pounds total

1 red onion, peeled and thinly sliced

¾ pound roasted red peppers (see page 171), cut into ½-inch strips

2 tablespoons julienned fresh mint leaves

3 cloves garlic, peeled and chopped

1 teaspoon grated lemon zest

Salt and freshly ground black pepper to taste

8 tablespoons extra-virgin olive oil

4 tablespoons red wine vinegar

Parlanno Siciliano

"SPEAKING SICILIAN"

A lot of snobs from up in the north might consider Sicily nothing more than an unfortunate appendage to the Italian nation and the Sicilian language merely bastardized Italian. The truth is that it's a noble nation within a nation, with its own beautiful language and culture. Sicilian is colorful, it's wacky, it has a poetic quality to it with a generous helping of humor and irony.

One of the things I love best about the Sicilians is that they are not ashamed to speak their own tongue. They gossip with their friends on the phone, they go to confession and tell the priest their sins, they go to the Korean vegetable market (because they know the Koreans have learned enough Sicilian to serve their customers), they scream at their mothers and kids, they make love to their wives and girlfriends—all in Sicilian. Up north, people might just speak their dialects among themselves, then standard Italian to anyone else. Not the Sicilians.

What does Sicilian sound like? Words often end in *u*, which is pronounced "ooh" but is a short "ooh" not a long, drawn-out one. The fish *merluzzo* easily becomes *merluzzu* and Brooklyn becomes *Bruccolinu*. Many times the *u* is added as a prefix. Basic grocery items such as *pane* ("bread"), *latte* ("milk"), and *sale* ("salt") become *upane, ulatte, usale*. Sicilian often adds a colorful twist to words, embellishing them with an extra syllable or two—a few extra consonants and vowels. *Carciofi* (car-*choff*-ee), a difficult enough word that means "artichoke," becomes *caccuociuli* (cah-*kwo*-chulee). Broccoli, the same in English and standard Italian, becomes *brocculeddu*. Garlic or *aglio* becomes *agghiu*.

Like other dialects, Sicilian is a spoken language, not a written one, and as such, proper grammar takes a backseat to expression. Some words are related to the standard Italian; others are completely different. Here are a few more:

spoon," used for cooking and occasionally for disciplinary purposes. If you were a kid with a tendency to misbehave, you had to watch out for that *paletta.* Just the threat of it was usually enough to keep you in line.

The culture and dialect of Sicily lend themselves especially well to proverbs. Sicilian proverbs are nuggets of ancient wisdom all wrapped up in word play and humor. They usually express a very definite opinion on a specific topic and they're often X-rated—or at least R. I'll give you a few PG ones here:

Chi practica con lo zoppo al anno zoppichia—If you hang out with a lame man, in a year you'll be limping, too.

Pani e sacramentu ci n'e'a ogni cunventu—Bread and sacraments are found in every convent (anyone can give you what you need).

Carni e pisci, a vita ti crisci—With meat and fish, you will live long.

Cu si marita, sta cuntentu un jornu; cu scanna u porcu, sta cuntentu un annu—He who marries is happy for a day; he who butchers a pig is happy for a year.

Cafe e vinu, cauri o friddi, ammazzanu i picciriddi—Coffee and wine, hot or cold, will kill the children.

Cu di vinu e'amicu, a iddu stissu e'nimicu—He who is too good a friend of wine is his own enemy.

ITALIAN	ENGLISH	SICILIAN
fagiolo	bean	*fazole*
sedano	celery	*acciu* (pronounced "achoo," like a sneeze)
prezzemolo	parsley	*petrosino*
uva	grape	*racina*
uva passa	raisin	*uvetta*
lumachina	sea snail	*babbaluci*

There are also words unique to Sicilian, important ones to know around the house. *La mappina* is the all-purpose "dishcloth" and "dishrag," an indispensable piece of equipment in the kitchen. *La paletta* is a "big wooden

Lucciariello

Sausage and Broccoli Pie

This is a wonderful closed pizza, for which you'll find a recipe in many a Sicilian kitchen, including that of Pasquale Verde and family, dear friends of ours who live in Castellammare. Patsie, as we called him, had some sense of humor. I remember the time he put a laxative in the chocolate dessert for a large group of guests at his home. To make matters worse, as in most small Sicilian towns in those days, the bathrooms were all outhouses!

1 recipe Pasta per Pizza (page 219)

12 ounces broccoli florets, separated into small pieces

4 tablespoons extra-virgin olive oil

2 cloves garlic, peeled and crushed

1 small jalapeño pepper, cut in half and seeded (see Note)

Salt and freshly ground black pepper

8 ounces Italian sweet sausage, removed from the casings and crumbled into pieces

2 large ripe tomatoes, thinly sliced

Preheat the oven to 425°F.

Divide the dough into 2 portions, 1 slightly larger than the other. On a lightly floured surface, roll out the larger piece into a 12-inch round. Then roll out the other piece into a slightly smaller round. Cover them with a damp towel and allow to rest for 10 minutes.

Cook the broccoli for 2 to 3 minutes or until tender in a pot of boiling salted water. In a skillet over medium heat, lightly brown the garlic in 2 tablespoons of the olive oil. Add the hot pepper and broccoli and cook for 2 to 3 more minutes. Lightly season with salt and pepper. Remove from the skillet and set aside. Add 1 more tablespoon of the olive oil to the skillet and brown the sausage in it. Add the broccoli to the sausage, check the seasoning, set aside, and allow to cool.

Spread the cooled mixture evenly over the larger round of dough and lay the sliced tomatoes on top. Cover with the smaller round, bring the edges over and seal them well. Brush with the remaining 1 tablespoon olive oil, place on a baking sheet, and bake in a preheated oven for 25 minutes, or until golden brown. Serve immediately.

Serves 6

Note: You can also use what we call an Italian hot pepper. In Italy, they call them *peperoncini*, but don't ask for that in the States because you'll get something completely different: the light green peppers that you find pickled in jars in all the supermarkets. Because of this confusion, I've called for a jalapeño, much easier to find in the United States, and there's no question about what it is.

Sfinciune

Sicilian-Style "Pizza" with Onions and Anchovies

The *sfinciune* is a Sicilian favorite that gets its name from the local word for "soft" or "light," in reference to its airy crust. You'll find many different versions of this dish in Sicily and this is one of my favorites. I have every reason to believe that this is the original deep-dish pizza. So there, Chicago!!

For the dough

1 cup warm water

1¼-ounce package active dry yeast

3 cups all-purpose flour

½ cup freshly grated pecorino romano cheese

1 teaspoon salt

¼ teaspoon freshly ground black pepper

3 tablespoons extra-virgin olive oil

For the sauce

5 tablespoons extra-virgin olive oil, plus extra for the pizza pan

1 large onion, peeled and thinly sliced

1 clove garlic, peeled and minced

3 large ripe tomatoes, peeled, seeded, and diced

2 anchovy fillets, chopped

2 sprigs fresh oregano, picked of its leaves

½ cup fresh bread crumbs

2 ounces caciocavallo cheese (you can substitute provolone), cut into ½-inch dice

TO PREPARE THE DOUGH: Combine the yeast and the warm water. In a separate bowl, combine the flour, pecorino romano, and salt and pepper. Make a well in the center and add the yeast mixture and 2 tablespoons of olive oil, mixing with a wooden spoon or in a mixer until you have a smooth elastic dough, about 8 minutes. Line a bowl with the remaining tablespoon of olive oil, place the dough in the oiled bowl, cover it with plastic wrap, and leave in a warm place for 1 hour until the dough doubles in size.

TO PREPARE THE SAUCE: Place 2 tablespoons of the olive oil in a saucepan over medium heat and sauté the onion and garlic for 10 minutes or until wilted and golden brown. Stir in the tomatoes, anchovies, and oregano leaves, and simmer for another 10 minutes. Reserve and allow to cool.

In a skillet over medium heat, sauté the bread crumbs in 1 tablespoon of the olive oil until golden brown.

Brush a pizza pan with some olive oil, roll out the dough, and line the pizza pan with it, allowing it to rise for another 30 minutes. Meanwhile, preheat the oven to 425°F.

With your fingertips, make dimples, ½ inch deep and 1 inch apart, all over the dough. Top the dough with half the sauce, spreading it to within ½ inch of the edge. Bake in the oven for 25 minutes.

Remove from the oven, spoon the rest of the sauce on top, sprinkle with the cheese, then with the bread crumbs, and drizzle with the remaining 2 tablespoons of olive oil. Bake in the oven for 8 minutes and serve.

If by any chance you have leftovers, the sfinciune is just as good reheated the next day.

Makes one 12-inch sfinciune

Pan di Ceci
con Salvia

Chickpea Flatbread with Sage

I first came across this recipe, which is incredibly easy to make and equally delicious, as part of an antipasto plate in Palermo. There's a variation of this bread in the province of Liguria, which includes the northwest coast of the Italian peninsula—the cities of Genoa, Portofino, and the spectacular Cinqueterre area. Up there they call the chickpea flour *farinata*. In America you can find it in specialty shops and Italian delis.

> **2 cups chickpea flour**
> **1½ cups cold water**
> **2 teaspoons salt**
> **⅓ cup extra-virgin olive oil**
> **6 fresh sage leaves**
> **Freshly ground black pepper to taste**

Place the chickpea flour in a bowl, slowly whisking in the water, salt, and olive oil. Cover and allow to stand at room temperature for at least 1 hour.

Preheat the broiler section of your oven and set the rack about 6 inches from the flame. Lightly coat a 13- x 9-inch baking pan with olive oil. Stir the batter and pour it into the pan. Break the sage leaves into large pieces and sprinkle them over the batter along with a generous amount of black pepper. Broil the batter for 5 minutes or until the top is lightly browned. Reduce the temperature to 450°F. and bake for an additional 5 minutes or until the bread pulls away from the sides of the pan. Cut into squares and serve immediately.

Serves 6

CACIOCAVALLO

Caciocavallo (kahtch-oh-cah-*vah*-loh) is a member of the family of *pasta filata* ("handmade stretched-curd") cheeses that includes mozzarella and provolone. It is made from cow's milk and often comes in a distinctive gourdlike shape (consisting of two connected balls, one larger than the other, with a string tied in the middle). Caciocavallo also comes in long thin cylinders and in large rectangular chunks. Like mozzarella, it has a mild, slightly salty flavor and a rich, smooth consistency. You can also buy it smoked or aged; in both cases it becomes stronger-tasting and harder or grainier in texture than its original state.

In most of America, authentic imported Italian cheeses are hard to come by and expensive. Many of the domestic versions are nothing more than bland factory-made imitations. Yes, they have real milk and so forth, but they aren't handmade and they just can't achieve the taste and texture of the real thing. My advice is to make the extra effort and seek them out.

zuppe

In southern Italy, as elsewhere throughout the world, soups are first and foremost comfort food meant to nourish you, drive away the chill, and pick you up when the elements are knocking you down.

Naples is part of the boot, and although some may disagree, it's much closer in a culinary sense to northern Italy than Sicily is. There has always been plenty of traffic between north and south, so it's no surprise that you'll find some recipes that originated up north served around Naples and Campania.

In Sicily, soups often call for dried ingredients—fava beans, wheat berries, split peas—that can be bought in bulk year-round, and are practical and economical. And this brings us to possibly the key point about soups: They're inexpensive, highly nutritious, and can feed the whole family from one pot, which has been extremely important to my frugal *compari* for many generations.

My grandmother Mary Lazzarino and her brother Pasquale Pesce on their communion day

Zuppetta di Cozze

Neapolitan Mussel Soup

What can I say about mussels? They're inexpensive, widely available, and absolutely delicious. Saffron, on the other hand, while readily available in the spice sections of supermarkets or in specialty stores, is expensive. The bad news is there is no substitute for it; the good news is a little bit goes a long way.

This recipe calls for cavatelli, one of my favorite pasta shapes. It is a short, thick, scalloped-edge shell. You can make cavatelli at home or buy it fresh or dried at the market. Any way, it's great—not just in a soup like this one but also with your favorite pasta sauce (see the next chapter).

This is a fantastic little soup (*zuppetta*), featuring the unbeatable combination of garlic, seafood, and tomatoes. When you finish eating it, you're going to jump up and yell "Beautiful!"

3 tablespoons extra-virgin olive oil

6 cloves garlic, peeled and crushed

1 anchovy fillet, chopped very fine

1 tablespoon capers, rinsed and chopped

¼ teaspoon fresh oregano leaves

¾ pound tomatoes, peeled, seeded, and coarsely chopped

2 cups Chicken Stock (page 216) (water is an acceptable substitute)

2 pounds cultivated mussels, well cleaned (see Note)

Pinch of saffron

⅛ teaspoon crushed red pepper flakes

10 ounces cavatelli

Salt and freshly ground black pepper to taste

Place the olive oil in a heavy-bottomed soup pot over medium heat. Add the garlic and sauté until lightly browned. Add the anchovy, capers, and oregano and sauté for 1 minute. Add the tomatoes, chicken stock, mussels, saffron, and red pepper flakes. Cover the pot and cook for 8 minutes.

While the mussels are cooking, cook the pasta in a large pot of salted water. When the mussels are cooked, remove them from the pot with a slotted spoon. Discard any unopened ones and remove the rest from their shells.

Drain the pasta, placing the shelled mussels back into the soup with the pasta, adjust the seasoning, allow to simmer for 3 to 4 minutes, and serve. Don't forget to provide plenty of crusty bread to mop up.

Serves 4 to 6

Note: To clean mussels, rinse them very well under cold running water, scrubbing lightly with a brush, and then pull off the little stringy "beards" that stick out of the shells. (Cultivated mussels don't have beards.) Do not use any whose shells don't stay closed.

Gnocchi di Ricotta in Brodo

Ricotta Gnocchi in Broth

Growing up, we ate many different items *in brodo*. These broth recipes are classic comfort food—quick and easy to make and warming to the heart. Gnocchi are always a nice touch, but the most important thing in this recipe is the broth. On occasion I'll allow you to substitute a good canned chicken stock, but for this you need to make a real old-fashioned homemade one. There are hundreds of variations on the recipe for basic chicken stock, one of which I offer in the Basic Recipes section of this book. If you have one you like better, by all means use it.

Gnocchi are one of the great unsung heroes of Italian cooking, by the way. Could that be because the word is so difficult for most Americans to pronounce? Just think of the combination "n" and "i" sound in the word *onion* (or in the Russian for "no," *nyet*) and there you have the key to pronouncing the word *gnocchi*—it's *"nyoh-cky"* not *"knocky."*

1 pound ricotta cheese, drained of excess water

2 cloves garlic, peeled and chopped

4 sprigs fresh Italian parsley, leaves only, washed and chopped

1 cup dried bread crumbs

2 cups freshly grated Parmesan cheese, plus additional for sprinkling

2 large eggs

Salt and freshly ground black pepper to taste

12 cups Chicken Stock (page 216)

1 cup tightly packed spinach leaves, cut into small pieces

Mix the ricotta, garlic, parsley, bread crumbs, Parmesan, and eggs in a bowl. Season with a little salt and pepper. Mix with a wooden spoon or in a mixer until it achieves the consistency of wet dough. Scoop the mixture out 1 teaspoon at a time and form it into tiny cigar-shaped dumplings. The recipe should yield about 30 dumplings (gnocchi).

Bring the chicken broth to a rolling boil, add the spinach, and drop the dumplings in one at a time. When they come to the surface, allow them to cook for an additional 2 minutes. Adjust the seasoning and serve the soup hot.

Serves 4

Passato di Ceci con Gamberi

Chickpea Soup with Shrimp

When I was a kid I had an Uncle Joe who was a master of Neapolitan-style cuisine. He lived in the Catskill Mountains and had a beautiful garden. All of his fresh produce made its way into his recipes. It was a treat to spend summers there. He had one strict rule, though: You had to eat what he cooked. If you didn't eat it for dinner, it was waiting for you the next morning at breakfast. In those days *ceci* ("chickpeas") were not one of my favorites. I would not eat them, by hook or by crook—for breakfast, lunch, or even dinner. One fine day Uncle Joe took pity on me, pureed them into a soup, and I've been hooked ever since. Here is my version of his recipe.

1 pound dried chickpeas, soaked in water overnight

1 medium white onion, peeled and chopped

3 fresh sage leaves

3 sprigs fresh Italian parsley

3 cloves garlic, peeled

3 sprigs fresh rosemary—always fresh!

3 tablespoons extra-virgin olive oil

Salt and freshly ground black pepper to taste

8 large shrimp, shelled, deveined, and cut in half lengthwise

Drain the chickpeas, place them in a large heavy-bottomed pot with the onion, sage, Italian parsley, garlic, and 1 sprig of the rosemary. Cover with water, bring to a boil, lower heat to a simmer, and cook for 1 hour or until the beans are tender.

While the soup is cooking, heat 2½ tablespoons of the olive oil with 1 more sprig of rosemary in a small saucepan over a medium-low flame for about 1 minute. Pass the oil through a strainer and reserve.

When the chickpeas are well cooked, remove the sage and rosemary. Reserve ¼ cup of the chickpeas for garnish and puree the rest in a blender until smooth. If you find the soup too thick, add a little water. Season with salt and pepper.

In a skillet over medium-high heat, cook the shrimp in the remaining olive oil for 1 minute, seasoning lightly with salt and pepper. Add the shrimp and reserved chickpeas to the soup and serve immediately, drizzling some infused olive oil and sprinkling a few rosemary leaves on top of each bowl.

Serves 4

GARLIC

When you're shopping for garlic, look for the bulbs with hard stem or neck portions; these are the most flavorful ones. Also, never buy bulbs that have sprouted, because they're beginning to turn bitter. American garlic has white skin and a stronger, sharper flavor, while Italian or Mexican garlic has a purplish skin and a milder flavor.

The easiest way to peel a clove of garlic is to crush it with the side of the blade of a large kitchen knife. Don't flatten it completely, just give it a good crunch. This loosens up the peel nicely so it can be removed easily. If you prefer, you can carefully hand-peel each clove with a small, sharp paring knife.

Minestra di Pesce

Seafood Soup with Fennel and Saffron

Every self-respecting regional cuisine of the Mediterranean has a version of fish soup. Whatever you call it—*zuppa di pesce, caciucco, brodetto, cioppino, (bouillabaisse* in southern France)—this is one of my favorites, melding the flavors of garlic and tomatoes with the local fresh seafood. I got this version from a friend of mine named Anthony Russo, a fisherman who plies the waters near the island of Capri. Anthony is a funny guy whose recipe originates with his mother. He loves garlic and calls it the most important vegetable in the world. He claims his mother wore a braid of garlic around her neck before going to bed at night to keep his father away!

You can add other shellfish, such as clams or mussels, as well as any number of different types of fish, depending on what's good and fresh and local.

1 whole porgy or other thick, firm, white-fleshed fish, about 2¼ pounds

1 small live lobster, about 1 pound

1 pound monkfish fillets

2 cups dry white wine

3 tablespoons extra-virgin olive oil

1 leek, washed very well (to remove any dirt or mud that's caked inside or out) and diced

1 medium onion, peeled and finely chopped

2 carrots, peeled and diced

1 celery stalk, diced

5 cloves garlic, peeled and crushed

1 bay leaf

2 sprigs fresh thyme

1 teaspoon fennel seeds

Generous pinch of saffron

2 cups canned peeled Italian plum tomatoes, with their juice, chopped (you can also use fresh tomatoes and peel them yourself)

Zest of 1 orange (cut into large pieces, not grated or chopped)

Salt and freshly ground black pepper to taste

4 jumbo shrimp (about U-4, see page 117)

Trim the fish by cutting off the head, tail, and any fins, and reserving the flesh. Kill the lobster by quickly inserting the point of a large knife into the top of the head, between the eyes. The lobster will die instantly. Cut the lobster's tail into two pieces and cut off the claws. Leave its head whole. Place fish trimmings and lobster head in a large soup pot, cover with 1 quart cold water, and bring to a boil over high heat. Lower heat and allow to simmer for about 12 to 15 minutes. Remove trimmings and heads and discard. Add the wine, olive oil, leek, onion, carrots, celery, garlic, bay leaf, thyme, fennel seeds, saffron, tomato, and orange zest and allow to simmer for an additional 15 minutes over very low heat. Remove the bay leaf, then pass everything through a food mill to create a smooth soup. Return to a simmer, add the reserved fish and the monkfish fillets, and season lightly with salt and pepper. Allow to simmer for 5 more minutes, then add the shrimp. Simmer for another 5 minutes and serve hot with some pieces of crusty bread for mopping up.

Serves 4

Vellutata di Cipollotti e Calamari

Silken Scallion Soup with Squid

When you think of featuring vegetables in a soup, I am sure that scallions don't jump to the top of your list. They can have a sharp, oniony flavor that sticks with you. Surprise, here's a cooking method that mellows the scallions, creating an irresistible blend of flavors. Note that the recipe calls for flour, which is normally not my favorite way to thicken a soup. In this case, though, it's exactly what eliminates the aftertaste of the scallions, highlights the subtle flavor of the calamari, and yields an unforgettably silky texture.

In Naples and throughout Campania, this is a recipe that's prepared using green onions, but I've adapted it for the United States, substituting scallions, which are much easier to find here.

3 tablespoons unsalted butter

1 pound scallions, green and white parts, thinly sliced

¼ cup all-purpose flour

6 cups Chicken Stock (page 216)

Salt and freshly ground black pepper to taste

¼ cup extra-virgin olive oil

1 shallot, peeled and chopped

1 bunch Swiss chard, washed and cut into 1-inch pieces

½ pound small squid, cleaned, the sacs cut into rings

½ cup peas (if fresh peas are not available, use defrosted frozen ones)

4 slices stale bread, cut into ¼-inch cubes

1 tablespoon chopped fresh Italian parsley

1 tablespoon chopped fresh basil

Heat the butter in a soup pot over medium-high heat, add the scallions, and cook for 2 minutes until softened. Sprinkle the flour over the scallions and continue to sauté for 2 more minutes. Add the stock, whisking continuously until all the flour is dissolved and there are no lumps. Season lightly with salt and pepper, lower the heat and allow to simmer uncovered for 45 minutes. Puree the soup in a blender or food processor until smooth.

Place 2 tablespoons of olive oil in a large skillet over medium heat and sauté the shallot for 1 minute. Add the Swiss chard, squid, and peas, cook for 3 to 4 more minutes or until the Swiss chard is wilted and the squid is opaque. Lightly season with salt and pepper.

Toss the bread cubes in the remaining olive oil and the herbs, then toast them in the oven at 400°F. for 3 to 4 minutes or until golden brown.

Add the squid mixture to the scallion soup and serve hot with the herb croutons on the side.

Serves 4

Zuppa di Santa Lucia

Wild Mushroom Soup

I love mushrooms any way you serve them—grilled, braised, in salads, and especially in soup. This particular soup is legendary in my family. We always said that when you taste it you can't help but sing. That's why they called it Santa Lucia—after the famous Neapolitan song.

Although I don't normally recommend using dried mushrooms, I call for dried porcini in this recipe since the fresh ones are very seasonal. Dried porcini mushrooms work well for soups, where their flavor—not the consistency or presentation—is the main concern.

1 ounce dried porcini mushrooms

7 tablespoons extra-virgin olive oil

1 medium onion, peeled and finely chopped

3 cloves garlic, peeled and chopped

2 pounds mushrooms, cleaned and sliced (cremini, portobello, shiitake, or oyster mushrooms will do)

5 fresh Italian plum tomatoes, peeled, seeded, and finely chopped

1 teaspoon salt

Freshly ground black pepper

1 sprig fresh marjoram

1 sprig fresh thyme

6 cups Chicken Stock (page 216)

3 large egg yolks

¼ cup grated Parmesan cheese, plus additional for sprinkling

1 tablespoon grated pecorino cheese

¼ cup chopped fresh Italian parsley

8 slices Italian bread, preferably stale, cut ½ inch thick

Soak the porcini in a cup of warm water for at least 30 minutes. Drain the liquid, straining it through a fine strainer to remove any sand. Reserve the strained liquid, rerinse the mushrooms, pat them dry, and chop them finely.

Place 4 tablespoons of the olive oil in a large soup pot over medium heat. Sauté the onion and garlic for about 5 minutes until wilted. Add the porcini and the white mushrooms and cook for 10 minutes. Add the porcini liquid, tomatoes, salt, pepper, marjoram, thyme, and the stock. Bring to a boil, lower heat, and allow to simmer for 15 minutes.

Combine the egg yolks, Parmesan, and pecorino in a mixing bowl, then gradually whisk 1 cup of the hot soup into the mixture to warm it. Then whisk the egg mixture directly into the simmering pot, stirring to thicken the soup. Add the parsley and cook for 5 more minutes.

Meanwhile, brush the slices of bread with the remaining olive oil and toast them in the oven at 400°F. until golden brown. Place 1 piece of the toast in the bottom of each serving bowl, ladle in the soup, and serve with additional grated Parmesan on the side.

Serves 8

La Frittedra

Artichoke, Fava Bean, and Pea Soup

This is a traditional Sicilian peasant dish that makes use of fresh fava beans, which have a delightfully subtle flavor and texture as well as a beautiful green color. They require some extra work in the shelling but it's definitely worth it. A staple in Sicily, fresh favas are something of a delicacy in America. They are available for a limited time in summer. If you cannot find them fresh, you can substitute dried ones, soaking and precooking them just like any other dried bean, and proceeding with the recipe. In Sicily, they're just as likely to use dried favas for this recipe but they're quite hard to find here, so I included the fresh ones. If you can't find either, substitute lima beans.

3 pounds fresh fava beans

3 tablespoons extra-virgin olive oil

1 medium onion, peeled and thinly sliced

6 artichoke hearts, fresh or frozen, cut into quarters

1 cup peas, fresh or frozen (never canned)

8 fresh basil leaves

Salt and freshly ground black pepper

Freshly grated pecorino romano cheese

Shell the fava beans by breaking each pod with your fingers, removing the beans, and then removing the leathery shell on each bean. (You can shell the favas easily by blanching them very briefly in boiling salted water, then making a small slit with your thumbnail where the two sides join, and then simply peeling back the shell.)

Place the olive oil in a soup pot over medium heat. Add the onion and sauté for 3 minutes or until golden brown. Add the fava beans, artichokes, peas, and basil. Lower the heat and allow to cook for 12 minutes, stirring periodically. Add enough water to cover the ingredients, raise the heat, and bring to a boil. Reduce the heat and allow to simmer for about 1 hour until the fava beans dissolve and the soup is thickened. Stir the soup as it cooks so that it doesn't burn the bottom of the pot. Season to taste with salt and pepper and serve with the cheese on the side for sprinkling.

Serves 4

Minestra di Cacuocciuli e Pasta

Artichoke and Pasta Soup

This recipe was a favorite of my father's Uncle Nino. He was a fun guy who loved to joke around and eat. In fact, he loved to eat so much that he weighed three hundred pounds. He also loved to travel, and during one of his trips, he went to the Vatican. As he walked around the Vatican he marveled at all the fabulous treasures. The place was overflowing with so much great artwork, they could hardly find places to hang it on the walls. Uncle Nino saw a cardinal walking around and, with appropriate reverence, remarked, "Your Holiness, this is unbelievable, all this art, all this wealth, do you realize that if you sold one painting, you could feed millions?" The cardinal, in all his knowledge and dignity, looked around for a second, turned to Nino, and said, "Get outta here, fatso!"

1 tablespoon extra-virgin olive oil

5 ounces pancetta, finely chopped

1 medium onion, peeled and finely chopped

2 cloves garlic, peeled and chopped

1 celery stalk, finely chopped

1 pound baby artichokes, trimmed of tough outside leaves and quartered (see Note)

2 ripe tomatoes, peeled, seeded, and finely chopped

8 cups Chicken Stock (page 216)

Salt and freshly ground black pepper

½ pound ditalini or other short pasta

2 tablespoons chopped fresh Italian parsley

¾ cup freshly grated pecorino cheese

Place the olive oil and pancetta in a large soup pot over medium heat and cook for 2 minutes, rendering the pancetta. Add the onion and garlic, and sauté for 3 more minutes. Add the celery and artichokes and sauté for 5 more minutes. Add the tomatoes and chicken stock, season with salt and pepper, bring to a simmer, lower the heat, and cook for 25 minutes.

Add the pasta and parsley and cook for 7 to 8 minutes or until the pasta is al dente. Serve the soup hot with the grated pecorino on the side for sprinkling.

Serves 6

Note: If fresh baby artichokes are not available, substitute frozen artichoke hearts. Do not use canned; they just don't taste good.

Pallottoline in Brodu

Tiny Meatball Soup

Everybody loves soup. Everybody loves meatballs. Therefore, everybody loves this recipe. Seriously, though, simple hearty soups like this one were one of the main foods for the poor immigrant families that came over from southern Italy and Sicily earlier this century. This was one of my family's favorite soups and it fed them on many a night when there wasn't much else to eat.

½ pound ground veal

3 tablespoons freshly grated Parmesan cheese, plus additional for sprinkling

4 tablespoons fresh bread crumbs

1 large egg

1 tablespoon chopped fresh Italian parsley

Salt and freshly ground black pepper

1 quart Chicken Stock (page 216)

½ cup cooked acini pepe pasta (or any other small pasta shape such as ditalini or even the tiny pastina)

Combine the veal, Parmesan, bread crumbs, egg, and parsley in a bowl, mixing very well. Salt and pepper to taste. Form into meatballs the size of marbles. Set aside on a plate.

Place the chicken stock in a large pot over medium heat, bringing it to a simmer. Carefully drop the meatballs into the stock and gently simmer for 5 minutes. Gently stir in the cooked pasta and allow it to cook for another 3 minutes. Ladle the soup into serving bowls and serve with some additional grated Parmesan on the side.

Serves 6

Minestra i Lenticchi

Lentil Soup with Macaroni

This dish is not to be mistaken for Pasta e Lenticchi, which is *not* a soup and which was in my first book, *Little Italy Cookbook*. Guess what? This one's definitely a soup. One tradition in Sicilian households is to eat lentil soup while walking up and down the stairs on New Year's Eve. Believe it or not, this is supposed to bring good luck. Leave it to the Sicilians! As a kid I remember my family doing it until one time my Uncle Tony joined in after indulging in another family tradition—drinking the homemade wine. After he gave Aunt Gloria a lentil soup bath, we started eating the soup sitting down. And after Tony got a wine bath from Gloria, he stopped drinking on New Year's Eve—or else!

½ pound pancetta, cut into small dice

1 large onion, peeled and thinly sliced

3 carrots, peeled and cut into small dice

2 celery stalks, cut into small dice

1 pound dried lentils, washed well and
　　drained

1 pound ditali or other small pasta,
　　cooked and drained

5 sprigs fresh Italian parsley, leaves only,
　　chopped

Salt and freshly ground black pepper
　　to taste

Extra-virgin olive oil for garnish

Freshly grated pecorino romano cheese

In a large soup pot over medium heat, sauté the pancetta for 2 to 3 minutes until lightly brown. Add the onion, carrots, and celery, cooking for another 5 minutes. Add 4 quarts of water and the lentils, bring to a boil, and lower the heat to a light simmer. Allow the soup to simmer for 3 hours, stirring periodically to ensure that it doesn't burn on the bottom. If it gets dry, you can add a little water.

When the soup is ready, stir in the pasta and the parsley and season with salt and pepper to taste. Allow to heat through about 5 minutes, then ladle into soup plates to serve, drizzling with the olive oil and serving the pecorino on the side.

Serves 6

Zuppa alla Gaddina Antica

Good Old-fashioned Chicken Soup

What mother or grandmother of any nationality under the sun doesn't have her own version of chicken soup? It's the perfect dish to nourish you when you're well and comfort you when you're sick. Here is the Sicilian version, *gaddina* being the term for *gallina* or hen. You'll note the addition of several finishing touches—the basil, Parmesan, and pieces of stale bread—that transform this soup into a characteristic Sicilian meal-in-a-bowl.

For the broth

1 chicken, about 3½ pounds

1 small carrot, peeled

1 celery stalk

1 clove garlic, peeled

1 small onion, peeled

10 sprigs fresh Italian parsley

Coarse sea salt to taste

For the soup

4 tablespoons unsalted butter

2 tablespoons extra-virgin olive oil

2 small carrots, peeled and finely chopped

1 celery stalk, finely chopped

1 small white onion, peeled and finely chopped

8 white mushrooms, cleaned and finely chopped

10 sprigs fresh Italian parsley, washed and finely chopped

¼ pound vermicelli, broken into quarters

Salt and freshly ground black pepper

To serve

8 slices stale Italian bread, cut 1 inch thick, brushed with olive oil and garlic, and toasted

15 fresh basil leaves, coarsely chopped

Freshly grated Parmesan cheese

TO PREPARE THE BROTH: Wash the chicken inside and out. Place it in a pot with the carrot, celery, garlic, onion, parsley, and 4 quarts of water over medium heat. Bring the water to a boil, add salt to taste, lower the heat, and simmer for 1 hour 30 minutes. Periodically skim the foam that forms on top of the broth.

Remove the chicken to a cutting board and strain the stock through a fine strainer. Skin and bone the chicken, discarding the skin and bones, and cut the meat into strips. Allow the stock to cool. The fat will come to the top where it can easily be skimmed off.

TO PREPARE THE SOUP: Place the butter and olive oil in a medium-size casserole over medium heat. When the butter is melted and begins to sizzle, add the chopped carrots, celery, onions, mushrooms, and parsley and sauté for 10 minutes, stirring periodically. Add the chicken, season with salt and pepper, and sauté for 4 more minutes. Add the broth and allow to simmer for 10 minutes. Add the vermicelli and simmer for 5 more minutes, stirring occasionally.

TO SERVE THE SOUP: Place a slice of toast in each serving plate, ladle the broth with the meat and vegetables on top, sprinkle with basil, and present with the grated Parmesan on the side for sprinkling.

Serves 8

Zuppa di Grano

Wheat Berry Soup

When I was a kid growing up in Brooklyn, we lived in a typical old brownstone with high tin ceilings, fireplaces, and long narrow rooms. It had an ancient coal furnace that took a long time to heat the place up. I remember many a cold winter morning when we would run into the kitchen where my grandmother would have the oven on with the door open to warm the room. It was on such mornings that my grandmother would make our favorite soups. This one was always at or near the top of the list.

Wheat berries are whole, unprocessed wheat kernels, popular in health-food circles these days. They are traditional in Sicilian cuisine, usually in sweets. And, as you will see, they make a great soup.

In Italian, the word *battuto* means something that's smashed or mashed down. It refers to a combination usually consisting of garlic and herbs chopped together on a cutting board, most often with a *mezzaluna* ("half-moon"), the typical curved, two-handled chopping blade. A *battuto* is often sautéed in olive oil to start off a recipe, but in this case it's used as a garnish.

1½ cups wheat berries, soaked in cold water overnight and drained

1 large white onion, peeled and finely chopped

3 celery stalks, finely chopped

3 cloves garlic, peeled and crushed

2½ pounds tomatoes, peeled, seeded, and chopped

6 cups Chicken Stock (page 216)

1 cup dry white wine

2½ cups precooked white navy beans (canned are an acceptable substitute)

Salt and freshly ground black pepper to taste

For the battuto crudo

¼ cup chopped fresh Italian parsley

¼ cup chopped fresh basil

2 cloves garlic, peeled and chopped

⅓ cup grated pecorino cheese

Place the wheat berries in a heavy-bottomed pot with the onion, celery, garlic, tomatoes, stock, and wine. Bring to a boil, lower heat, and simmer for 30 minutes, covered.

Stir in the beans and simmer for 10 more minutes or until the berries are tender. Season with salt and pepper.

TO PREPARE THE BATTUTO: Combine all the ingredients, mixing well with a spoon.

Serve the soup, sprinkling an equal portion of the battuto over each serving.

Serves 6

Zuppa di Piseddi Secchi e Patate

Split Pea and Potato Soup

My father's great aunt, Angelina, used to make this soup for us when we were young. Which reminds me of a story. Have you ever heard about how protective Sicilians are of their daughters? It's all true. Angelina was so protective of her daughter Josie, it was ridiculous. When her daughter was finally allowed to date her future husband, the family would walk twenty feet behind them wherever they went. They dated for nine years and were only able to kiss during the last year. When they finally got married, my aunt insisted they have the honeymoon at her house. Their first night, my aunt didn't sleep a wink. Whenever it got quiet, she would yell, "Hey, whatsa going on inna there?" Then she started to eat the biscotti—crunch, crunch, crunch—all night. Needless to say, my cousins didn't have their first child till they were married for five years.

> ½ pound split peas, rinsed well
>
> 1 medium carrot, peeled and cut into
>   medium dice
>
> 2 medium potatoes, peeled and finely
>   chopped
>
> 5 cups Chicken Stock (page 216)
>
> 4 tablespoons extra-virgin olive oil
>
> 1 medium onion, peeled and finely chopped
>
> 1 clove garlic, peeled and finely chopped
>
> Salt and freshly ground black pepper
>
> 3 tablespoons freshly grated Parmesan
>   cheese

Place the peas, carrot, potatoes, and 3 cups of the stock in a soup pot over medium heat and cook until all the ingredients are very tender. Puree the soup in a food processor or blender until very smooth.

Place the olive oil over medium heat in a separate skillet and sauté the onion and garlic in it until golden, about 4 minutes. Add the contents of the skillet to the soup pot along with the remaining stock. Allow to simmer for about 10 minutes, stirring constantly. Season with salt and pepper, add the grated Parmesan, and serve.

Serves 6

The Sicilian Character

I really love the Italians' sense of identity. Gather a sampling of Italians from all over the country, put them in a room, go around one by one and ask them if they're Italian, and you'll get almost as many different answers as there are people in the room.

With a true native, the conversation goes something like this, "You're Italian, right?" "No, I'm Sicilian." Likewise with the Calabrese, Abruzzese, Neapolitan, and so forth. Another typical conversation: "Oh, *madonn'!* My sister's gonna marry a Neapolitan! What are we gonna do?" "Well, you could start by trying to talk her out of it." And these aren't people right off the boat. These are second- and third-generation descendants like me, some of whom have never set foot in Italy! Yet they still consider themselves Sicilians, Neapolitans, Calabrians, and so on.

The Sicilians are something else. You've heard the expression "crazy like a fox"? Well, that goes a long way toward describing the Sicilian character. Some of them, if you look at them the wrong way, might never speak to you again—or worse. They have long memories; they know how to hold a grudge. You don't want to make enemies with a Sicilian. On the flip side of that coin, they have many enviable qualities—loyalty, strength, stoicism in the face of incredible pain and difficulty. They possess an indomitable spirit and ingenuity. Actually, my father embodies a lot of these qualities and I guess a few might have rubbed off on me. . . .

In one breath, I'll tell you there is no such thing as a typical Sicilian; in the next, I'll tell you my father is a typical Sicilian, my uncles and aunts are typical Neapolitans. I know, generalizations breed stereotypes, stereotypes breed prejudice, and the Italians, particularly Sicilians, have suffered from this. That's not just or fair, especially applied to such a group of rugged individualists. On the other hand, stereotypes exist for a reason. Why not celebrate the positive ones and not worry too much about the negative ones? Here are some Sicilian traits. I know they're true because I've observed them:

Your word is your deed—You say what you mean and you do what you say. Sicilians have a low tolerance for BS. They will tell you straight up what they think to the point of being harsh. Outsiders shouldn't misinterpret this blunt honesty as rudeness.

Loyalty—There are two types of people in the world: friends and everybody else. Sicilians are loyal, maybe sometimes to a fault. If a friend calls you and says "I need a thousand dollars right away" or "I gotta sleep in your house tonight because my wife threw me out," you do him the favor, no questions asked.

Elephants have nothing on them—Sicilians never forget; they *might* forgive but they don't ever forget. When you hurt them, they don't necessarily strike back in reaction. They wait and do it when you least expect it. Whoever said revenge is a dish best served cold must have had the Sicilians in mind. A Sicilian might not talk to a relative for forty years because of a small perceived insult. As you can imagine, this makes it very difficult to plan the seating charts for weddings.

Working things out—This principle is represented by the phrase *cia rangiamo* (pronounced cha-*rahn*-jah-moh), meaning "We'll work something out" or "We'll make an arrangement." No matter how thorny the problem, how messy the situation, Sicilians believe there is a way to fix it. They also have a natural generosity, a tendency to want to help other people. Whether it's unexpected guests for dinner or real-life issues, a Sicilian will find a way to make things right.

Discretion—Don't hang your dirty laundry out for everyone to see; only trust people who are really your friends. You might chitchat or gossip about inconsequential day-to-day matters but you practice utter discretion in matters of true importance.

Toughness, stoicism—Sicilians are survivors. They know life can be a struggle. They've been through a lot, they're resilient. Remember, over the centuries they were conquered by everybody within spitting distance—Greeks, Romans, Saracens, Normans, Aragons, Germans.

pasta

Seated are my great-grandmother's parents, Antoinette and Michelle Quagliariello; her sister Mary stands behind her mother

You'd be hard pressed to find a family in Naples or Sicily that doesn't eat pasta once a day. Because they prepare it so often, they've come up with endless variations, both in terms of macaroni shapes and types of sauces. The recipe for Gemelli al Pappone would be a good example of both. The *gemelli* ("twins") are a fairly unusual shape while the sauce is a clever, contrasting combination of crispy fried zucchini and basil cream sauce. Then you've got your classic traditional pasta dishes, which should never be ignored. They may seem like clichés, but they're clichés for a reason—because they're elegantly simple and incredibly delicious. I try to offer a sampling of these with the occasional twist, for example, a linguini with white clam sauce punctuated by the addition of some pancetta.

For the most part, pasta is served as the opening course in a multicourse Italian meal. On special occasions—a Sunday meal or a big feast—it may be preceded by an appetizer. In this country, I think a lot of people have formed a false impression that Italians regularly eat huge helpings of pasta followed by several more large courses of meats, vegetables, and desserts. Nothing could be further from the truth! The quickest way to insult an Italian is to plop down a huge plate of macaroni swimming in sauce. In America, we have a tendency to misconstrue the term *abbondanza*, which has nothing to do with making a pig of yourself. We tend to believe that more is better, that the restaurant serving the biggest portions is superior. In Italy, the pasta course, when served after the antipasto and before the entrée, consists of no more than what we would consider a half portion. The most common mistake, other than overcooking the noodles, is adding too much sauce.

The farther south you go in Italy, and particularly in Sicily, the more you see baked pasta dishes that are more akin to casseroles—Penne alla Norma, for example, or the Timballo di Mulinciani e Pasta. These dishes are heartier, more substantial, and so they're more likely to become entrées or main courses in kitchens on both sides of the Atlantic.

The couple on the right is my great-grandmother and -grandfather Antoinette Quagliariello and Andrea Pesce

A Few Choice Words on Cooking Pasta

Cooking pasta just right is a skill so basic, yet so crucial to achieving an authentic and satisfying Italian cuisine that nobody should ever take it for granted. How many times has it been written—an eloquent description of how to cook pasta perfectly al dente, just the other side of undercooked, so it retains its shape and texture without turning to a mushy, starchy mess? And how many times have inattentive cooks—even the most accomplished amateur and professional chefs—ignored the instructions and overcooked it? It's something so simple, yet so easy to screw up.

The most common error is to cook the pasta perfectly then return it to the hot pot and leave it there. Even after the flame has been turned off and the pasta drained, it continues to cook, especially if it's resting on a hot stove. Timing is everything. You need to plan ahead, estimate the cooking time of the particular shape you're using, and be there to test for doneness while it cooks. Don't expect to walk away and come back to a perfectly cooked pot of pasta. Depending on the size and thickness of the pasta, it will take anywhere from 6 or 7 to 14 minutes to cook. Follow the instructions on the packet but trust your own instincts and experience even more. Sometimes the instructions say 12 minutes but you know it cooks in 10.

The minute your pasta is cooked—and that may be well under your original estimate—you had better spring into action: Drain it, transfer it to a bowl, toss it with the sauce, and serve. That bowl of pasta and sauce should hit the table steaming hot so all of its delicious aromas can fill the dining room and enhance that wonderful moment of anticipation before it's passed around the table and served into plates or bowls. If your friends or family aren't ready, seated at the table, that's their loss. You shouldn't have to chase them around the house and herd them to their places while you're trying to put food on the table.

Dried pasta is always cooked in generously salted water that is first brought to a rolling boil. Certain beliefs to the contrary, there is absolutely no need to put any oil in the water; simply stir the pasta to prevent it from sticking to itself and/or the pot. You've got to be there while it cooks so you may as well stir it.

Pasta needs a relatively large amount of water to cook in; the classic rule of thumb is to allow 5 quarts for each pound of

Genera Quagliariello

pasta being cooked. Into these 5 quarts, you should toss a good handful of salt. You can cover the pot to help bring the water to a boil more quickly, but leave it uncovered while cooking the pasta or you'll risk having it overflow and making a big mess on your stove.

The ratio of sauce to pasta is also very important. It can be difficult to judge, but it's always better to toss the macaroni with a little less sauce at first. You can always add more later. The pasta is supposed to be the main event, the sauce an embellishment. You want to achieve a balance tilted somewhat in favor of the pasta.

The sauce and the pasta should always be tossed just before serving so that the pasta is lightly and evenly coated. Serving the sauce in a mound on top of each plate of pasta looks pretty, but that's about it: Sometimes that's how they do it in restaurants to impress people with their presentation.

Fresh pasta should be plunged into boiling water for about 2 to 3 minutes. Be extra careful to test it constantly so you don't overcook it. It may cook in under 2 minutes and once you've over-done it, there's no going back.

Cavatelli al Sugo di Pollo

Cavatelli Pasta with a Chicken Ragù

As you may recall from the mussel soup recipe in the previous chapter, cavatelli is one of my all-time favorite pasta shapes. It's good dry but better yet if you can find it fresh or frozen. It has great texture, and most important, it holds the sauce very well. When I was a kid, even if my grandmother made another type of pasta, she would often treat me to a plate of cavatelli on the side. This sauce is something a little different—with the chicken—and it's the perfect complement to the cavatelli.

3 tablespoons extra-virgin olive oil

1 chicken, about 3½ pounds, cut into 16 equal-size pieces

3 red onions, peeled and chopped

Pinch of crushed red pepper flakes

2 pounds very ripe fresh tomatoes, passed through a food mill

2 tablespoons tomato paste

2 large pinches of saffron

21 fresh basil leaves, julienned

Salt and freshly ground black pepper

1 pound cavatelli

Freshly grated pecorino romano cheese

Place the olive oil in a large heavy-bottomed pot over medium-high heat and sauté the pieces of chicken until golden brown on all sides, about 12 minutes. Remove the chicken pieces with a slotted spoon. Add the onions to the pot, along with the red pepper flakes, and cook them for 10 minutes or until translucent. Add the tomato and the tomato paste, mixing well. Add the saffron and allow to simmer for 3 to 4 minutes. Return the chicken to the pot, along with the basil, and lower the heat, allowing the sauce to simmer for 30 minutes. Season with salt and pepper.

While the chicken is simmering, cook the pasta, drain it, mix well with the sauce, and serve with the grated pecorino on the side.

Serves 8

Pecorino

Aside from the undisputed king, which is Parmesan, Italy has many other great cheeses, and pecorino is one of them. In Italian, *pecora* is the word for "sheep." Pecorino, therefore, is ewe's milk cheese.

There are several excellent types of pecorino from different regions of Italy. In Tuscany, they make a superb one, which comes two ways: "fresh," or aged. The fresh is mellow, medium-hard, and creamy. The longer the cheese is aged, the sharper, drier, and saltier it becomes. Once a cheese becomes hard enough to grate, it's referred to as *grana*, a general term for "hard and grainy." If you go into an *alimentari*, or "grocery store," in Italy and ask for *grana*, you're likely to be given a Parmesan-type cheese, although probably not the superior name-controlled Parmigiano-Reggiano. You might also be handed a piece of aged pecorino.

The most famous pecorino in Italy is *pecorino romano*, often shortened to just plain Romano. The genuine article is made only in the province of Rome, but there are many imitations. It is a dry, very sharp, and salty cheese that's mostly used in place of Parmesan—for grating on top of pastas, soups, and other dishes. There is also a very fine pecorino from the island of Sardinia, called *pecorino sardo*. A delicious traditional summer snack or appetizer is pecorino with fresh fava beans. The rich, salty, mildly chalky cheese is a perfect foil for the fresh, green, crunchy beans. With a piece of good home-style bread, it makes an unbeatable picnic.

Of course I'm prejudiced, but my favorite pecorino is the *pecorino siciliano*. It comes in several variations. One is *incanestrato*, or *canestrato*, which means "basketed"—so called because the curds are drained of their whey in a basket and the cheese keeps a telltale crisscross pattern on its outside. *Pepato* is a version of pecorino that has a horizontal layer of black peppers through its middle.

A NOTE ABOUT OLIVE OIL

Extra-virgin olive oil, the rich dark-green oil that is the most expensive, highest grade can be used in any of the recipes in this book. The next grade down, which is labeled "pure olive oil" and is a cheaper, lighter, more refined product, is called for in many of the recipes that involve frying or sautéing. In these cases, extra-virgin is not necessary and you can save some money by using the pure grade. When extra-virgin is called for, however, don't skimp. You will be taking away from the ultimate flavor and texture of the dish.

Conchiglie al Sugo di Carne

Shells with Sausage and Cream Sauce

Conchiglie (con-*kee*-lee-eh) means "seashells" in Italian. If you're having problems convincing your kids to eat a healthy plate of pasta, try grabbing their attention by explaining the shapes—seashells, butterflies, bow ties, pens, little ears, even "priest-stranglers" *(strozzapreti)*.

2 tablespoons pure olive oil

1 tablespoon unsalted butter

2 tablespoons very finely chopped onion

½ pound luganega sausage, removed from the casings and crumbled (see Note)

Salt and freshly ground black pepper

⅔ cup heavy cream

1 pound conchiglie

Freshly grated Parmesan cheese

Place the olive oil and butter in a skillet over medium heat. Melt the butter, and when the foam subsides, add the onion and cook until golden. Add the sausage and cook for an additional 10 minutes. Season lightly with salt and pepper, add the cream, and stirring frequently, cook until the cream is thickened.

Cook the pasta al dente, drain well, and toss with the sauce. Serve immediately with some freshly grated Parmesan on the side for sprinkling.

Serves 4

Note: Luganega sausage is thinner in diameter than standard Italian sausage and comes coiled up in a spiral.

Gemelli al Pappone

Gemelli with Creamy Zucchini and Basil Sauce

Zucchini is a wonderful, healthy, ubiquitous vegetable that's easy to grow in your garden and available in abundance at any market. Frankly, though, in most recipes it has a tendency to seem ordinary. Furthermore, when you try to incorporate it into a sauce it turns to mush and disappears. This old Neapolitan family recipe is quick and delicious and it makes use of zucchini in a more interesting way, frying it until golden and crispy—which allows it to maintain its integrity—then incorporating it into a creamy sauce where it provides good textural contrast.

- **1 pound zucchini**
- **Canola oil for frying**
- **1 pound gemelli**
- **3 tablespoons unsalted butter**
- **2 tablespoons extra-virgin olive oil**
- **1 teaspoon all-purpose flour, dissolved in 1 cup milk**
- **Salt and freshly ground black pepper**
- **⅔ cup coarsely chopped fresh basil**
- **1 large egg yolk, beaten**
- **¼ cup freshly grated Parmesan cheese**
- **½ cup freshly grated pecorino romano cheese**

Wash the zucchini well and cut into sticks 3 inches long and ⅛ inch thick. Place canola oil in a heavy-bottomed pan to a depth of ½ inch over medium-high heat. Fry the zucchini sticks until golden brown on all sides. Drain well on paper towels.

Cook the pasta al dente. While the pasta is cooking, melt half the butter with the olive oil in a skillet. Stir in the milk and flour mixture. Add the zucchini, salt and pepper, and the basil, stirring constantly. Cook for about 3 minutes, then remove the skillet from the heat and stir in the remaining butter. Stir in the egg rapidly, finishing the sauce with the grated cheese.

Drain the pasta, toss well with the sauce, and serve.

Serves 4

Ragù

The Famous Sunday Gravy

What can I say? When I was growing up, it was never "sauce," it was always "gravy." It was never "pasta," it was always "macaroni." This is my grandmother's world-famous gravy, featuring four different kinds of meat and long, slow cooking. *Madonn'!* I would kill for this stuff. It was always the first thing I'd smell when I woke up on Sunday mornings. Then I'd go to the kitchen, break a piece of fresh Italian bread, which, by the way, was always sitting on top of the refrigerator, and dip it in the gravy.

This sauce is one of the great treasures that the Neapolitans brought with them to America. In Naples, they call it *ragù*. If you asked my grandmother where she got the recipe, she'd say, "My mother." If you asked her mother, she'd say, "My mother." You get the picture.

A final thought: My grandmother always measures the water using the tomato and tomato-paste cans.

¼ cup plus 3 tablespoons extra-virgin olive oil

7 cloves garlic, peeled and thinly sliced

Six 6-ounce cans tomato paste

12 tomato-paste cans water

Three 35-ounce cans whole tomatoes, with their juice, pureed and strained of seeds

1½ tomato cans water

2 sprigs fresh oregano, leaves only

1 teaspoon salt

9 fresh basil leaves

⅛ teaspoon crushed red pepper flakes

1 recipe Polpetti (page 138)

1 recipe Bracciole di Maiale (page 133)

¾ pounds beef stew meat, cut into large cubes

1 pound Italian sausage (sweet or hot or a combo—take your pick), cut into 1½-inch pieces

Place the ¼ cup of the olive oil in a very large heavy-bottomed sauce pot over medium heat. Sauté the garlic for about 1 minute or until slightly golden. Add the tomato paste and fry it with the garlic for 5 minutes or until the paste is bubbling, constantly stirring so as not to burn it. Stir in the 12 tomato-paste cans of water and allow to simmer for 20 minutes or until thick.

Add the pureed tomatoes, the 1½ tomato cans of water, the oregano, salt, basil, and red pepper flakes. Bring to a boil, then lower the heat so that the sauce barely simmers. Place a wooden spoon under the cover to keep the pot partially opened.

While the sauce cooks, place the remaining olive oil in a large skillet over medium-high heat and begin to brown the meats evenly on all sides.

After the sauce has been simmering over low heat for 2 hours, add the meats, being careful not to break the meatballs. Make sure the meats are completely covered by the sauce and continue to cook for 1 to 1½ more hours, stirring periodically, always careful not to break the meatballs. When the sauce is ready, skim the excess oil from the top, adjust the seasoning, and serve with long fusilli, a pasta that will get a knowing look from real Italians.

Makes 6 quarts

Rigatoni al Pomodoro e Basilico

Rigatoni with Tomato and Basil

Olive oil, garlic, tomatoes . . . like Gehrig, Ruth, and DiMaggio, it's the heart of the lineup when it comes to any type of Italian cooking, from Little Italy all the way over to the Bay of Naples and the coastline of Sicily. Start with this holy trinity, sprinkle with a little Parmesan, and you're in heaven.

What I love about this type of recipe is that you can give these basic ingredients to ten different chefs and they'll come up with ten different sauces. It all boils down to the quality of the ingredients and restraint. The best chefs have a light touch and the ability to discipline themselves by holding back. They know how to let the ingredients really shine and not get too fancy. This is the kind of classic dish that pasta is all about.

¼ cup extra-virgin olive oil

1 medium white onion, peeled and chopped

3 cloves garlic, peeled and chopped

¼ cup chopped fresh Italian parsley

One 28-ounce can whole peeled plum tomatoes, with their juice (you can also use fresh tomatoes, peeled, seeded, and chopped)

½ cup julienned fresh basil leaves

Salt to taste

1 pound rigatoni

1 cup freshly grated Parmesan cheese

Place the olive oil and the onion in a sauce pot over medium heat. Cook for 2 to 3 minutes until the onion is translucent, add the garlic, and cook for another 2 to 3 minutes, being careful not to brown the garlic. Add the parsley and the tomatoes with their liquid, breaking them up with a wooden spoon. Raise the heat to medium-high and cook the sauce, stirring frequently, for about 30 minutes, at which point it should be thickened considerably. Puree the sauce in a food mill, blender, or food processor. Return the sauce to the pot over medium heat, add the basil and cook for approximately 5 more minutes. Season with salt to taste.

Cook the pasta al dente. Drain, toss it with the sauce, and serve immediately with the Parmesan cheese on the side for sprinkling.

Serves 6

The Neapolitan Dialect

If you want to cook the food, you've got to delve into the culture, which means the music and the language, the beauty of the country and its people. I'm not saying you can't cook authentic Italian without taking a Berlitz course, just that you need a flavor of things before you ever go into that kitchen. A lot of us second- or third-generation types may not know how to speak much proper Italian, but we've got a feel for our dialects deep in our hearts and souls; the sounds, the rhythms, and the patterns are a part of us that I want to share with you.

There are a lot of similarities between Neapolitan and Sicilian. You'll notice different words, different variations on standard words, but the spirit is the same. Both dialects are spoken with humor, gusto, a love of life, a sense of humor, and an appreciation of life's struggles and ironies. If you ever visit the city of Naples—or any other place where its natives live in significant numbers—you'll immediately sense the street theater that is Neapolitan life. All the screaming, yelling, bluffing, cursing, pleading, cajoling, and fooling around—all the little dramas—are part of an innate expressiveness that is played out in the dialect.

In Neapolitan dialect, they shorten the words; the phrases are blunt and direct, and they put little embellishments on certain expressions, as they do in Sicilian, albeit with a different twist. *Andiamo ce'ne* (ahn-dee-*a*-moh cheh-*neh*), which means "let's go," becomes *iamo c'en* (yah-mu-*gen*). *Vuoi andare* (vuoy ahn-*dar*-rey)? "do you want to go?" becomes vuo-i (*voh-ee?*)? *Dov'e?* ("where is," pronounced dohv-*eh?*) becomes *a'do'e* (ah-doe-*eh*)? Like Sicilian, Neapolitan is almost impossible to spell. In pronunciation, there's a tendency to drop the ubiquitous final vowel.

A few examples of Neapolitan words: Eggplant, *melanzana* in standard Italian, becomes *mulignane* (pronounced moo-lin-*nyan*); tomato, *pomodoro*, becomes *pomorolo*; zucchini is *cucuzielle*; mussels, *cozze*, are *cozziche*; parsley, *prezzemolo*, is *prutusina* (very similar to the Sicilian *petrosino*); likewise, celery, *sedano*, becomes *l'accia* (la-cha), which is very close to the Sicilian *acciu* (achoo); basil, *basilico*, is transformed into the more mellifluous *a'vasinicola*; artichokes, *carciofi*, are abbreviated to *carcioffol* in Neapolitan, whereas in Sicilian they become *caccuocioli*.

Neapolitan has a lilting, romantic, singsongy aspect and so it naturally lends itself well to song. One of the most famous songs, after "Santa Lucia" of course, is Mario Merola's rendition of "Che Bello a'Magna'," a hilarious ditty about stuffing your face, whose title translates roughly as "It's Beautiful to Eat." Try to find a recording and play it while you're cooking some of my food.

A few more phrases, just to give you a flavor:

Brutt' comm' o' peccat' (*broot* coe-mo pay-*caht*)—Ugly as sin.

Nu' sputa ngiel ca facc' te torna (nuh-*shpoot* n-jell kah-*fatch* teh-*torn*)—Don't spit into the wind (literal translation: Don't spit into the sky, it'll come back in your face).

A cchiu furb' e na volpe (ah-*cue* foorb eh-na volp)—Crazy like a fox (literal translation: Smarter than a wolf).

Malata comme' nu cane (mah-*lah*-tah koh-may new-*cah*- nay)—Sick as a dog.

Doldo' s'mang buon acca'tuorn (*dol*-doh seh-*mahnge* buohn acka-*torn*)—Where can you get a good meal around here?

Piscator' chi pigliatu? (*Peesh*-kah-tor key *pee*-lyah-too)—Hey, fisherman, what did you catch?

Penne ai Carciofi

Penne with a Savory Artichoke Sauce

Artichokes are a popular vegetable all over Italy and there is often a tremendous abundance of them in season, which is where recipes like this come in handy. I don't know about you, but the artichoke flavor is one of my favorites. Like fennel, it is unique, immediately recognizable, and maybe not to everybody's liking—either you love it or you don't. The nice thing about this type of recipe is that it brings the artichoke's subtle flavor to the forefront rather than masking it.

Artichokes are not so common in much of the United States, which means they can be expensive, particularly at the beginning and end of their season. The good news is you can substitute frozen artichoke hearts (even the three- and four-star chefs in France where I trained do it) and the dish still excels. Whatever you do, don't buy canned artichokes—they taste like metal. And don't ever cook artichokes in an aluminum or cast-iron pan because they also take on the taste of the metal that way. One final word: Try this sauce on grilled chicken. It's *delizioso*!

½ pound dried fava beans, soaked overnight

Coarse sea salt

4 large artichokes

1 lemon

5 ounces prosciutto, diced

10 ounces sweet Italian sausage, removed from the casings

3 cloves garlic, peeled

20 sprigs fresh Italian parsley, leaves only

½ cup extra-virgin olive oil

1 pound ripe plum tomatoes, peeled, seeded, and chopped

1⅓ cups Chicken Stock (page 216)

Salt and freshly ground black pepper

1 pound penne

Freshly grated Parmesan cheese

Cook the fava beans in salted boiling water for 30 minutes, shell them, then soak them in lightly salted water for another 30 minutes. Clean the artichokes by removing the tough outer leaves and the hairy inner chokes. Squeeze the lemon into a bowl of cold water large enough to hold all the artichokes. Cut the artichokes into 1-inch cubes and soak them in the lemon water briefly to prevent them from turning black.

Combine the artichokes, prosciutto, sausage meat, garlic, and parsley and coarsely grind in a meat grinder or food processor. Place the olive oil in a saucepan over medium heat and sauté the ground ingredients for 15 minutes, stirring. Add the tomatoes, drained fava beans, and stock, season with salt and pepper, and cook for another 30 minutes or until the fava beans start to dissolve.

Cook the pasta al dente, drain, mix with the sauce, and serve with the Parmesan on the side.

Serves 8

Palle di Tagliolini

Crispy Stuffed-Pasta Dumplings

Here is a recipe that I created, inspired by all the scrumptious little fried treats they feature in southern Italy and Sicily. Let's face it, people just love dumplings. You have your potato dumplings, your semolina dumplings . . . well, these are a little unusual in that they call for tagliolini, thin pasta noodles, mixed with balsamella and cheese, to form the dough. You can have some fun with the savory stuffing, substituting chopped sausage meats for the ham or even making it with shrimp. This dish works equally well with the pasta course or as an antipasto.

For the filling
4 ounces unsalted butter
4 ounces tiny green peas, fresh or frozen
Salt and freshly ground black pepper
5 ounces thinly sliced prosciutto, diced
1¾ cups coarsely grated mozzarella cheese

For the pasta
21 ounces fresh tagliolini
1 recipe Balsamella (page 216)
1¾ cups freshly grated Parmesan cheese
¼ cup fresh Italian parsley, chopped
3 large eggs
Canola or other light vegetable oil for frying
Fresh bread crumbs for garnish

TO PREPARE THE FILLING: Place all the ingredients in a bowl with ½ cup of the balsamella; mix well and set aside.

TO PREPARE THE PASTA: Cook the pasta in a pot of salted boiling water for about 1 minute, drain well, and return it to the cooking pot. Combine 1½ cups of the balsamella mixture with the Parmesan and parsley and add it to the cooking pot. Mix well and allow to cool, stirring periodically so the mixture doesn't stick to the pot. Beat the eggs in a separate bowl and pour them into the pot with the pasta, stirring well.

Take small handfuls of the pasta dough and form them into little pancakes. Place a large tablespoonful of the filling in the center of each pancake, then mold the pancake around the filling to form a sphere-shaped dumpling. Place the dumplings on a plate and continue to form and fill new ones until you've used all the filling mixture.

Place oil to a depth of 2 inches in a heavy-bottomed pot over medium-high heat. Place the bread crumbs in a shallow dish and roll each dumpling in the bread crumbs to cover. Fry the dumplings in the oil until golden brown all over, 4 to 5 minutes. Drain them well on paper towels and serve hot.

Makes 16 dumplings

Spaghetti Carbonara

Tina DiRosa's Spaghetti Carbonara

If you read my first book, you'll recall Tina's husband, Luigi, who is pastry chef and supervisor at Alba's Pastry Shop on Eighteenth Avenue in Brooklyn. Tina works at Alba's, too, and while he is Sicilian and she is Neapolitan they understand each other just fine. We shot a segment for my TV series at Luigi and Tina's house, and she prepared this recipe. It was incredibly delicious and what I loved most about it was that it didn't have any cream, whereas the traditional Spaghetti Carbonara is usually loaded with it—sometimes overloaded. For many years, Tina's family owned the famous restaurant Zi Teresa in Naples and this is how they used to make the carbonara there. Tina's version calls for bacon, rather than pancetta, because she feels it imparts more flavor.

2 sticks salted butter

4 tablespoons extra-virgin olive oil

1 large onion, peeled and chopped

1 pound sliced bacon, diced

8 links sweet Italian sausage, with casings, coarsely chopped

6 ounces dry white wine

2 pounds spaghetti

5 large eggs

6 tablespoons freshly grated Parmesan cheese, plus additional for sprinkling

Salt and freshly ground black pepper to taste

Chopped fresh Italian parsley

Melt the butter and olive oil in a deep skillet over medium heat, making sure the butter does not burn. Add the onion to the skillet and sauté until golden, 5 to 10 minutes. Add the bacon to the skillet and cook until it begins to melt, about 15 minutes. Add the chopped sausage and continue to cook until the meat is done, about 20 minutes. Add the white wine, raise the heat, and cook until the wine is evaporated.

While you prepare the sauce, cook the spaghetti al dente in an 8-quart pot. Drain the pasta and reserve 2 cups of the cooking water. Place the reserved cooking water in the skillet with the sauce over a low flame until thoroughly heated, 5 to 10 minutes. Meanwhile, beat the eggs in a bowl with the 6 tablespoons of cheese and salt and pepper. Place the drained spaghetti on a warm serving platter or in a large bowl and pour the juices from the skillet on top. Mix well, then stir in the egg-cheese mixture, add the solids from the skillet, mix well, sprinkle with parsley and the extra cheese, and serve.

Serves 8

Linguine ai Frutti di Mare

Linguine with Seafood

The greatest place in the world to enjoy this classic dish is by the Bay of Naples with the island of Capri in sight and the profile of Mount Vesuvius off in the distance. The atmosphere is perfect: the aromas of the sea, the ocean breeze, the cloudless sky. This is truly heaven, especially for me, who grew up near Coney Island in Brooklyn. If you don't know Coney Island, it was rumored that there were German subs off the beaches during World War II, but nobody ever saw them because they were destroyed by the pollution.

Frutti di mare, translates literally as "fruit of the sea." Of course what is meant is assorted fresh seafood. The fruit part tells you that it's fresh and plump, which it will be . . . if you go to the right places and demand the best.

½ **pound littleneck clams**

½ **pound cultivated mussels (see Headnote, page 93)**

½ **cup extra-virgin olive oil**

2 cloves garlic, peeled and crushed

⅛ **teaspoon crushed red pepper flakes**

2 cups canned Italian plum tomatoes, with their juice, coarsely chopped (you can also use fresh tomatoes, peeled and seeded)

½ **pound medium shrimp, peeled and deveined**

2 tablespoons chopped fresh Italian parsley

1 pound linguine

Salt and freshly ground black pepper

Scrub the clams and mussels under cold water and remove the stringy beards from the mussels (if necessary). Discard any clams or mussels that do not remain closed.

Place the olive oil in a saucepan over medium-high heat. Sauté the garlic until golden brown. Add the red pepper flakes and tomatoes, and cook for 3 minutes. Add the clams and mussels, lower the heat to medium, cover and cook for 3 to 4 minutes or until the clams and mussels open. Discard any that don't open. Add the shrimp and parsley, and cook for 2 more minutes.

Meanwhile, cook the linguine al dente, then drain very well. Add the linguine to the saucepan, season with salt and pepper, toss, and serve immediately.

Serves 4

CHEESE AND FISH?

There is a lingering belief, which you will encounter especially in Italy, that seafood is *never, ever* to be garnished with grated cheese. It's like an ancient taboo: To violate it is considered totally sacrilegious. Well, I have one word for that: *Baloney!* Do whatever you like. If you have a nice dish of pasta with seafood and Parmesan is your pleasure, who cares! For my show on the cable TV Food Network, I did an interview with some hardcore "Eye-talians" and, guess what, they put cheese on their seafood risotto. I'm not even sure of the origin of this taboo, but maybe it's because when shrimp starts to go bad it smells sour, like cheese. Whoever says you don't want cheesy tastes with fish is full of it. The French have been combining Gruyère with fish for years and I guess they know a thing or two about cooking. How about Lobster Thermidor? It's got cheese and it's delicious! If some waiter pulls a snob act on you and won't bring you cheese for your seafood pasta, then you get up and walk right out of that restaurant. I eat grated cheese on my linguine with red clam sauce and you have my permission to do it, too.

Spaghetti alle Vongole

Spaghetti with White Clam Sauce

Who doesn't love clam sauce, especially a white clam sauce? In Italy it's made with tiny little clams, no bigger than your thumbnail, called *vongole.* They are wonderfully sweet, tender, and tasty, but unfortunately difficult to find in the United States. You might come across some imported ones, but if not, use littlenecks, Manila clams, or even cockles. Whatever type of clam you use, enjoy the dish. If you dare sprinkle Parmesan cheese on it, though, I promise I will come to your house and harass you! (Just kidding.)

In testing this dish, I created a variation by adding the pancetta. You'll find it really adds something special to the final result and you have my permission to use it as your secret ingredient.

2 dozen of the smallest littlenecks you can find

½ cup extra-virgin olive oil

3 ounces pancetta, diced

2 teaspoons chopped garlic

¼ teaspoon crushed red pepper flakes

¼ cup dry white wine

1 pound spaghetti

1 teaspoon chopped fresh Italian parsley

1 teaspoon unsalted butter

Salt and freshly ground black pepper

Wash the clams very well under cold water.

Place the olive oil in a heavy-bottomed pan over medium heat, add the pancetta, and cook for about 1½ minutes. Add the garlic and red pepper, cook for about 1 minute, then add the clams, stirring frequently. After another minute or 2, add the wine, cover the pan, and allow it to cook for about 4 minutes or until the clams have opened.

As the clams are steaming, cook the spaghetti al dente.

When the clams have opened, remove them from the pan with a slotted spoon. Discard any unopened clams and keep the rest warm (leave in the pan, covered, off the heat). Add the parsley to the juice at the bottom of the pan and stir in the butter. Adjust the seasoning with a little salt and a generous amount of freshly ground pepper. Drain the pasta well, toss it with the clams and sauce, and serve immediately.

Serves 4

Spaghetti ai Gamberi

Spaghetti with Shrimp

Shrimp are one of those foods that people can't seem to get enough of. Ditto pasta. So when you pair the two of them, you have an instant winner. This is a simple, straightforward recipe that depends on one thing and one thing only: The shrimp must be absolutely fresh. If not, fuh-ged-aboud-it!

4 tablespoons extra-virgin olive oil

1 medium carrot, peeled and finely chopped

1 small onion, peeled and finely chopped

2 cloves garlic, peeled and finely chopped

18 sprigs fresh Italian parsley, leaves only, finely chopped

1 cup dry white wine

1½ pounds ripe plum tomatoes, peeled, seeded, and chopped

¼ teaspoon crushed red pepper flakes

1 pound spaghetti

1 pound medium shrimp, peeled and deveined

Salt and freshly ground black pepper

18 sprigs fresh Italian parsley, finely chopped

2 cloves garlic, peeled and finely chopped

Place the olive oil in a large skillet over medium heat. Add the carrot, onion, garlic, and parsley, and sauté for 10 minutes. Add the wine and cook for about 12 minutes. Add the tomatoes and red pepper, lower the heat, and allow to simmer for 20 minutes.

While the sauce is simmering, cook the pasta al dente.

Add the shrimp to the sauce for about 2 minutes, seasoning the sauce with salt and pepper to taste. Combine the parsley and garlic. Drain the cooked pasta, combine it with the sauce, sprinkle the garlic-parsley mixture on top, toss well, and serve.

Serves 6

San Marzano Tomatoes

NOTHING BUT THE BEST!

On the fertile, sun-drenched plain just to the south of Naples, they grow some of the best tomatoes in Italy, if not the world. The growers and wholesalers, the truckers, the packing factories, and the market—every segment of the tomato industry—is represented in and around the hub, San Marzano. The silhouette of Mount Vesuvius looms in the north. To the southwest lies the peninsula of Sorrento, with its steep rocky cliffs soaring thousands of feet up from clear blue waters; to the southeast, the rugged mountains of Irpinia, beginning at Avellino and continuing down past Sant'Angelo dei Lombardi, my ancestral homeland.

Italian resourcefulness and industriousness are on plentiful display in the towns and villages around San Marzano. Like much of Italy, the area is crowded and chaotic, full of life and very productive. If you look out over the valley from the mountains above, you see the roofs of the hundreds if not thousands of greenhouses. Called *serre*, they protect the precious crops from harsh winter winds. The growers, big and small, raise a little bit of everything. You might find a four-acre family plot, with Mom and Pop, Grandpa, and the kids tilling the soil and tending fifteen crops, right next to a state-of-the-art twenty-five-acre spread of greenhouse tomatoes or peppers.

There's no doubt that San Marzano tomatoes are absolutely the best for making sauce. Some confusion begins to arise, though, when you realize San Marzano is both a variety of tomato and the name of the principal town in the growing zone. In other words, you can have San Marzano tomatoes from San Marzano or San

Marzano tomatoes from San Valentino Torio nearby, but you can also have Roma tomatoes from San Marzano.

Roma and San Marzano are both types of plum tomatoes, so called because of their more or less oval shape. Most of the plum tomatoes we see in the United States—ripe or canned—are the Roma variety. The San Marzanos have a slight indentation at their waist and they come to a little point at the bottom. They are skinnier, narrower, not as plump and juicy as the Romas. They have more meat, less seed and pulp. But the crucial difference, most experts agree, is that they're not as sweet.

Because the dark volcanic soil of the San Marzano area is so rich in nutrients and also provides superior drainage (aeration and filtering), the tomatoes ripen a lot faster there than anywhere else. It can take as little as two months for a San Marzano plant in San Marzano to grow a full complement of ripe tomatoes whereas in your backyard it might take three months or more.

Further confusion may arise about why so many fine Italian recipes call for canned tomatoes at all—instead of fresh ones. It's not that we're looking for a shortcut, but due to the characteristics of the variety and the soil it is grown in, it is actually possible to achieve superior quality in a can. That's right, more often than not the genuine San Marzano tomatoes in a can are going to yield a better sauce than the fresh plum tomatoes you buy at the store.

Fusilli 'Ninsalata

Pasta Salad with Olives and Capers

When Geri and I got engaged to be married, she decided to cook a meal for our two families. It would be a great way for everybody to get acquainted. She prepared this salad to please my father. Everyone was there, all on their best behavior, ever fearful of my Sicilian father: no off-color jokes, no meatballs thrown.

My father sat at the head of the table. After eating Geri's pasta salad, he tapped his fork on his glass. There was a hush in the room. No one dared utter a peep. In his own brand of English, he said, "I wanna aska Geri a question. If it'sa one herb inna da whole worl', which is the besta for da man?" I quickly translated: "Geri, my father wants to know if you had to pick one herb in the whole world, what would be the best one for a man?" Everyone stopped eating, all eyes turned toward Geri. She scanned the room, realizing this could be an important moment—possibly the most important of her whole life. She took a deep breath and said, "Basil?" There was a pause that seemed to stretch out for minutes. . . . Finally, my father slammed his fist on the table and proclaimed, "She's-a right!" There was a burst of applause, the music started again, and Gino the dog passed out.

The spiral fusilli, by the way, are an excellent pasta shape for a salad because all their little nooks and crannies become deliciously coated with sauce and/or dressing.

¼ cup fresh mint leaves

¼ cup fresh basil leaves (see Note)

2 tablespoons fresh Italian parsley leaves

2 cloves garlic, peeled

Juice of 2 lemons

½ cup extra-virgin olive oil

1 large sprig fresh oregano

1 pound fusilli

½ cup diced fresh Italian plum tomatoes

12 Sicilian olives, pitted and cut into quarters

1 tablespoon capers, rinsed very well

To make the dressing, chop the mint, basil, parsley, and garlic in a food processor. While the motor is still running, squeeze in the fresh lemon juice, drizzle in the olive oil, pick the oregano leaves off their stems, and stir in. Set aside in a bowl.

Cook the fusilli al dente. Rinse under cold water until cool, then drain well. Add the fusilli to the bowl along with the tomatoes, olives, and capers. Pour on the dressing, toss well, garnish with the basil top if using, and serve at room temperature.

Serves 4

Note: If possible, reserve one large basil top (the flower) from a sprig to garnish the salad.

Pasta e Ceci

Pasta and Chickpeas

Whatever you call them—ceci, garbanzos, or chickpeas—when I was a kid, my grandmother begged, bribed, and threatened me to eat them to no avail. But she got my attention and at some point I underwent a miraculous conversion (page 32). Now I love them. Chickpeas with pasta is a traditional Sicilian dish that has Middle Eastern roots. Swiss chard, which is called *biete* in Italian, is not necessarily traditional, but in Salemi, near Castellammare, there was an old lady named Antonetta, a good friend of the family, who showed me this delicious recipe, so I adapted it. You could say it's a Sicilian version of pasta-fazool.

Remember to plan ahead because the chickpeas must be soaked overnight and cooked for 2 hours or more.

> **2 cups dried chickpeas (see Note)**
>
> **2 sprigs fresh rosemary**
>
> **3 cloves garlic, peeled**
>
> **1 large celery stalk, diced**
>
> **1 red onion, peeled and diced**
>
> **1 small carrot, peeled and diced**
>
> **Salt and freshly ground black pepper
>   to taste**
>
> **1 pound Swiss chard, cut into ¾-inch strips**
>
> **1½ cups broken-up spaghettini or any short
>   pasta shape you'd use for soup**
>
> **¼ cup extra-virgin olive oil**
>
> **2 tablespoons chopped fresh parsley**

Soak the chickpeas in a pot of cold water overnight. Drain them, clean the pot, and return the chickpeas to the pot. Add water to cover by at least 2 inches. Tie the rosemary together and

You can pit olives individually by lightly crushing them under the flat side of a large knife, which causes the pit to almost squirt out. If you have a lot of olives to pit, wrap them in an old but clean dish towel (one you don't mind staining a bit). Then crush them under the weight of a large pan or salad bowl. Unwrap the towel and pick out the pits. You can also use a plastic Ziploc bag in place of the towel.

add it along with the garlic, celery, onion, and carrot. Cover, bring to a boil, and simmer over low heat for 2 to 2½ hours or until the chickpeas are tender. Remove the rosemary and discard.

Puree ¾ of the chickpeas in a blender or food processor, then return them to the pot. Season well with salt and pepper, add the chard and the whole chickpeas, and cook for 3 minutes until the chard is wilted.

Cook the pasta in salted water until al dente, drain, add to the pot, and mix it all up. Ladle into individual bowls, drizzle with the olive oil, sprinkle with the parsley, and serve.

Serves 6

Note: If you want to take a shortcut, you can substitute canned chickpeas and simply mix them in with the rosemary, garlic, celery, onion, and carrots, then continue.

Pasta con le Sarde

Pasta with Sardines

No self-respecting Sicilian cook is without a recipe for this dish. If Sicily were a country, this would be top contender for the national dish. Until recently, fresh sardines were virtually nonexistent in fish markets outside the shores of the Mediterranean. You had to rely on canned ones. Now you should be able to obtain medium-size fresh sardines from your fish market, but you may have to specially order them in advance.

This particular recipe was shown to me by my Aunt Philomena. Like other Sicilian women, not only did she have a mustache but also a mole with a two-inch black hair growing out of it. As kids, we use to take turns trying to sneak up on her and pull it! And, man, could she cook.

Perciatelli are thick, hollow spaghetti. A similar shape is *bucatini*, which means "the little hollow ones."

½ pound fresh medium sardines, filleted

9 tablespoons extra-virgin olive oil

2 cloves garlic, peeled and chopped

One 6-ounce can tomato paste

1 sprig fresh oregano, leaves only

5 fresh basil leaves

3 tablespoons golden raisins

3 tablespoons pine nuts, lightly toasted

**Salt and freshly ground black pepper
     to taste**

**1 medium bulb fresh fennel, stem portions
     on top trimmed off (see Note)**

1 pound perciatelli

½ cup unseasoned bread crumbs

Freshly grated pecorino romano cheese

Cut the sardine fillets into 1-inch pieces. Place 6 tablespoons of the olive oil along with the garlic in a large saucepan over medium heat and sauté until the garlic is lightly golden brown. Add the sardines and continue to sauté, stirring until they form a paste, about 8 to 10 minutes.

Add the tomato paste along with 3¾ cups water to the saucepan, bringing the mixture to a boil. Add the oregano, basil, raisins, and pine nuts, lower the heat, and season with salt and pepper to taste. Simmer the mixture until it is thick, about 45 minutes.

As you begin to cook the sauce, place a large pot of water with a teaspoon of salt over high heat. Bring to a boil, then place the fennel bulb in it and cook for 45 minutes. Lower the heat and simmer until the fennel is tender. Remove the fennel, dice it, and add it to the sauce.

Keep the fennel water boiling in the pot and cook the pasta in it. Drain well and remove to a warm serving platter.

While you're cooking the pasta, place the remaining olive oil in a pan over medium heat and sauté the bread crumbs until golden brown, lightly seasoning them with a little salt and pepper.

Toss the pasta with the sauce, sprinkle it with the bread crumbs, and serve with the cheese on the side.

Serves 4

Note: When shopping for fennel, look for the shorter, rounder bulbs rather than the slender, long ones (which means the plant was overgrown). The squat, firm bulbs have the true fresh fennel texture and flavor.

Pasta con 'Scarola

Pasta with Escarole

In Brooklyn we never called it escarole, it was always 'scarole and we usually had it with beans, a staple of Little Italy cuisine. This recipe, pairing it with pasta, is one of my favorites and a great way to introduce you to 'scarole if you've never had it.

Escarole is actually a close relative of chicory and Belgian endive. It looks a lot like a slightly elongated head of lettuce with somewhat wavy leaves. It has a firm texture and a very pleasant, mildly bitter taste—just enough to make it interesting, but you won't notice any bitterness when it's cooked.

Look for the younger, smaller, more tender heads of escarole. If you can't find 'scarole, you can always substitute chicory, which has a lot of smaller curly leaves sticking out from the lettuce-type core. By the way, 'scarole is also great raw in a salad; any bitterness is nicely balanced by the oil-and-vinegar dressing.

1 pound tender escarole leaves, trimmed and washed well

½ pound spaghetti (you can substitute orecchiette or any other pasta shape you like)

½ cup extra-virgin olive oil

7 cloves garlic, peeled and chopped

¼ teaspoon crushed red pepper flakes

3 ripe tomatoes, peeled, seeded, and chopped

Salt and freshly ground black pepper to taste

Freshly grated Parmesan cheese

Cut the escarole leaves in half and cook them in a large pot of boiling salted water for about 8 minutes or until tender. Remove the escarole, reserving the water in the pot.

Break the spaghetti in half, then break the halves in half again. Bring the escarole water back to a rolling boil and cook the spaghetti in it until al dente. Drain, reserving 1½ cups of the water.

Place the olive oil in a large saucepan over medium-high heat and sauté the garlic until golden, about 2 minutes. Add the red pepper and tomatoes and allow to simmer for 4 minutes. Add the escarole, reserved water, and pasta and allow to simmer for another 4 minutes or until the escarole is hot. Season with salt and pepper and serve with the grated Parmesan on the side.

Serves 4

Pezze della Nonna

Grandmother's Stuffed Pasta Squares

I love this dish. It's one of those recipes that has been handed down from mother to daughter for hundreds of years. Yes, it's somewhat involved but it's also really fun and shows off the artistry of Sicilian home cooking. One fine feature is the tomato sauce, developed especially for this recipe. Another is the fresh pasta. If you don't have time to make it fresh in your own kitchen, you can buy it in premade sheets.

Pezze, by the way, means "pieces," so the recipe title translates, literally, as "pieces of Grandma." Actually, it refers to the stuffed pasta squares that are folded in exactly the same way that you would fold a "pocket square" or handkerchief—the two bottom corners in, then once more corner in, leaving a triangular peak on top.

For the tomato sauce

4 tablespoons extra-virgin olive oil

1 medium onion, peeled and chopped

1 celery stalk, chopped

2 cloves garlic, peeled and chopped

1 carrot, peeled and chopped

8 sprigs fresh Italian parsley, leaves only, chopped

8 large fresh basil leaves, chopped

2½ pounds ripe Italian plum tomatoes, roughly chopped

Salt and freshly ground black pepper

1 recipe Balsamella (page 216)

For the stuffing

2½ pounds fresh spinach, stems removed

Coarse salt

1 pound ricotta cheese, drained very well

1 large egg

3 large egg yolks

1 cup freshly grated Parmesan cheese

Freshly grated nutmeg

Salt and freshly ground black pepper

For the pasta

2¼ pounds all-purpose flour

4 large egg yolks

¼ cup cold water

2 tablespoons extra-virgin olive oil

Pinch of salt

TO PREPARE THE TOMATO SAUCE: Place the olive oil in a heavy-bottomed sauce pot over low heat and sauté the chopped onion, celery, garlic, and carrots for 12 minutes. Add the parsley, basil, and tomatoes, cover the pot, and allow to simmer for 45 minutes, stirring periodically so it doesn't burn on the bottom. When it's done, pass the sauce through a food mill, season to taste with salt and pepper, and keep warm (in a covered pot on the stove off the heat) or reheat later.

Prepare the balsamella according to the recipe and keep it warm.

TO PREPARE THE STUFFING: Wash the spinach well, drain, and blanch it in boiling salted water for 3 minutes. Refresh under cold water, drain well, and squeeze dry. Chop the spinach fine and place it in a bowl with the ricotta, egg, egg yolks, and Parmesan. Mix well, add the nutmeg, and season with salt and pepper. Set aside at room temperature, or if you make it ahead, refrigerate until ready to use.

continued

TO PREPARE THE PASTA: Place the flour in a bowl and make a well in the center. Place the egg yolks, water, olive oil, and salt in the well and mix with the flour until all ingredients are incorporated. Don't overmix. Allow the dough to rest for 15 minutes, then roll it out on a floured surface to a thickness of 1/16 inch. Cut the dough into sixteen 6-inch squares and cook them in a large pot of boiling salted water for about 30 seconds, then refresh them in a bowl of cold water. Transfer the pasta squares to a damp towel.

Preheat the oven to 375°F.

Lightly oil a baking dish large enough to hold all the pezze, slightly overlapping. Place 2 tablespoons of the stuffing in each of the pasta squares, fold it into a triangle, then take the two side ends and fold them to meet along the bottom edge. Place all the stuffed pezze in the baking dish, then pour the balsamella on top and bake in the oven for 15 minutes. Remove from the oven, spoon the tomato sauce on top, and serve immediately.

Serves 8

Penne alla Norma

Penne with Eggplant, Tomato, and Ricotta Salata

I'm sure the first thing you need to know is how this wonderful dish got its name. It's a famous old Sicilian recipe that originated in the area of Catania on the eastern coast of the island. As the story goes, somebody tried this new recipe and as a compliment to the chef exclaimed that it was as good as *Norma*, the local composer Vincenzo Bellini's operatic masterpiece that was topping the charts around the same time.

Now, the ricotta salata cheese that makes this recipe so special can be found in most Italian groceries. If you can't find it, don't worry. Buy regular ricotta and strain it in cheese cloth or a coffee strainer, in the fridge, for twenty-four hours to remove all excess water. The results will be similar. The point, with this step and the toasting, is to dry up the cheese and make it gratable.

For frying the eggplant, use the grade of olive oil labeled "pure," a lighter, generally yellower version more suited to frying.

One 7-ounce piece ricotta salata

4 tablespoons extra-virgin olive oil

1/2 small onion, peeled and chopped

3 cloves garlic, peeled and chopped

1/2 teaspoon crushed red pepper flakes

3 1/2 pounds ripe Italian plum tomatoes, peeled, seeded, and chopped

1/4 cup julienned fresh basil leaves

4 small eggplants

Salt

Pure olive oil for frying

Freshly ground black pepper to taste

1 pound penne

Preheat the oven to 200°F.

Toast the ricotta on a baking sheet until golden on all sides, about 15 minutes. (Turn it over after the first 7 minutes.) Allow the cheese to cool then grate it coarsely and set aside.

To make the sauce, place 3 tablespoons of the extra-virgin olive oil in a skillet over medium heat and sauté the onion for 4 minutes or until soft. Add the garlic and red pepper flakes and sauté for 3 more minutes. Add the tomatoes and allow to simmer over low heat for 20 minutes. Puree the sauce, stir in the basil, and reserve.

Trim the bottoms and tops off the eggplants, then cut them lengthwise into ¼-inch-thick slices. Lightly salt the eggplant slices and place in a colander with a bowl on top to press them down. Allow to stand for 30 minutes. Place pure olive oil to a depth of ¼ inch in a heavy-bottomed skillet over medium heat. Fry the eggplant until golden brown on both sides, turning once. Drain well on paper towels and season with fresh pepper.

Raise the heat in the oven to 350°F.

Cook the penne al dente. Drain the pasta well, toss it with three quarters of the sauce and half the cheese. Place a layer of the pasta in a baking dish, covering it with a layer of the fried eggplant slices. Layer the remaining pasta on top and then the remaining eggplant on top of that. Sprinkle the eggplant with the remaining cheese, and drizzle with the remaining sauce and 1 tablespoon of olive oil. Bake in the oven for 5 minutes and serve.

Serves 6

RICOTTA

The Italian word *ricotta* means "recooked" and this cheese is so named because it is actually made from the whey or liquid that is a by-product of making other cheeses. This by-product was once a problem—it stunk up the sewers and encouraged the growth of all kinds of molds and bacteria— until some smart cheesemaker discovered you could make more cheese from it. All you had to do was heat it up and extract the new curds that were formed.

Ricotta salata is the salted, dried version and the best of it comes from Sicily, although they also make it in other parts of southern Italy. Authentic ricotta salata is pressed from sheep's milk whey, dried, lightly salted, then aged for at least three months. The harder, longer-aged version can be used for grating onto pasta. It provides a flavor that is a little stronger than Parmesan and a little milder than pecorino romano.

The regular nonsalted ricotta is milder and can be made from cow's, sheep's, or goat's milk. The best type of ricotta, which can be difficult to find, is made from bufala mozzarella whey.

Castellammare del Golfo

If you saw the town today you would wonder why anybody would ever want to leave. *Castellammare*, which means "castle by the sea," is at the end of a long sweeping crescent of coastline that defines the gulf of the same name. It has a small harbor protected by the ancient fortress that juts out into the bay.

I have fond memories of trips to Castellammare as a kid. My father still owns a house there and every time I go back I'm struck by the beauty and serenity of the place. That doesn't mean it isn't a hard life for the people there and it certainly was hard in the days when my first ancestors left to seek better fortunes in America. Nowadays, Castellammare is a sleepy fishing village that relies partly on tourism for its livelihood.

One of my favorite memories of Castellammare is the custom the old ladies have of making tomato paste. They set up a big, thick iron pot right out in the street, build a wood fire under it, and boil those tomatoes down all day, long and slow, until they have a thick concentrated paste.

I also remember hiking up into the brown, grass-covered hills behind the town. We'd pick wild berries in the thickets up there. Sometimes we'd see tough-looking guys, called *lupi* ("wolves"), with the traditional visored caps and shotguns slung over their shoulders, herding a few sheep.

Timballo di Mulinciani e Pasta

Timbale of Eggplant and Macaroni

One of my grandmother's brothers was named Pasquale. He was in the army and they sent him to Texas. Poor Pasquale—in those days hardly anybody in Texas had ever seen an "Eye-talian," let alone figured out how to say his name. So he became "Pat." My grandmother used to send care packages to him, including salamis, cheeses, breads, and this timbale, to make sure he would survive the experience. Then one day the sergeant told them to knock it off because the olive oil was dripping all over the rest of the mail.

This dish looks great and it has that extra added taste-and-texture bonus of the browned bread crumbs on top.

2 medium eggplants

Salt

3 tablespoons unsalted butter

½ cup bread crumbs

Pure olive oil for frying (see Note)

1 pound perciatelli

3 cups of your favorite tomato sauce or Marinara Sauce (page 217)

2 large sprigs fresh oregano, leaves only

3 tablespoons chopped fresh basil

½ cup freshly grated Parmesan cheese, mixed with ½ cup grated pecorino romano cheese

Freshly ground black pepper

Peel the eggplants and slice them lengthwise about ⅜ inch thick. Place them in a colander and sprinkle liberally with salt. Allow them to sit for at least 1 hour. The salt will draw much of the moisture out of the eggplant and, along with it, any bitterness. Pat dry.

Coat a 10-inch springform pan with 1 tablespoon of the butter and line it evenly with 2 tablespoons of the bread crumbs.

Brown the eggplant slices in the olive oil on both sides. Drain the slices well on paper towels. Line the bottom of the mold with eggplant slices in an overlapping pattern. Lay more slices, overlapping, around the sides of the mold, leaving some overhang. Reserve enough slices to create a top layer on the mold once it's filled with pasta (see below).

Preheat the oven to 350°F.

Cook the pasta in salted boiling water, leaving it somewhat undercooked. (It will cook more in the oven.) Drain the pasta well, return it to the pot, stir in 2 cups of the tomato sauce, the oregano, basil, and cheese. Season with salt and pepper to taste. Spoon the pasta into the mold, fold over any excess eggplant, and cover the mold with the remaining eggplant slices. Press down very well, sprinkle with remaining bread crumbs, dot with the remaining butter, and bake in the oven for 25 minutes or until golden brown. Heat the remaining 1 cup of tomato sauce.

Remove the pan from the oven, place a platter on top, and invert the pan to remove the *timballo.* Serve hot with the remaining sauce on top.

Serves 8

Note: The eggplant slices will need to be fried in several batches. They soak up a lot of olive oil; count on about 2 to 3 tablespoons per batch.

frutti
di mare

Holding the cigar, my mother's father, Leonard Lazzarino

Naples is home to a busy port; it's a transportation hub, a crazy bustling city, a major center for tourism, but its clear blue waters also harbor a tremendous variety of fish and shellfish.

Seafood is as basic to Neapolitan cooking as olive oil, garlic, and tomatoes. In fact, many of the recipes are variations on that fundamental three-note theme. However, as simple and down-to-earth as these recipes are, without crisp timing and impeccable freshness of ingredients, they won't live up to their glorious potential.

Sicilian cuisine is *dominated* by seafood and most of Sicily's population of about five million live by the sea. Their fish markets are a sight to behold, exhibiting an abundance of big oceangoing fish, namely, tuna and swordfish. There are also plenty of fresh sardines, which, at about six to eight inches long, are much bigger than the canned variety we see in America.

When buying fish, remember, fresh fish does not smell fishy. It has a very faint odor of the sea—just a hint of that salt-air freshness borne on a gentle breeze off the ocean. (One thing, it should never smell like low tide at Coney island!) Keep fish on ice right up to the moment you're ready to prepare it. Its skin should be shiny and clean, not slimy. Its eyes should be clear, not cloudy.

The wedding in Sant'Angelo dei Lombardi of cousin Carmela Novelli to Andrea Lauria

Calamari Ripieni di Gamberi

Squid Stuffed with Shrimp

Nature could not have created a creature better designed for stuffing than the humble squid. Once you clean it, which, by the way, your local fishmonger will be delighted to do for you, you've got the sac for stuffing and the tentacles for chopping, frying, sautéeing, and so forth. Squid has a very mild flavor and, prepared correctly, a wonderful tender texture with little fat. Shrimp—well, everybody knows their rich taste—and the combination is a good study in complement and contrast.

10 squid, 6 to 7 inches long

1 pound medium shrimp

⅔ cup extra-virgin olive oil

2 cloves garlic, peeled and chopped

2 tablespoons chopped fresh Italian parsley

⅓ cup bread crumbs, lightly toasted in a skillet

Salt and freshly ground black pepper to taste

1¼ cups dry white wine

Wash the squid and soak in a bowl of ice water for 30 minutes.

While the squid are soaking, shell and devein the shrimp, washing them well in cold water and cutting them into large dice.

Remove the squid from the water. To clean the squid, separate the tentacles and the attached innards by pulling them carefully but firmly away from the body. Cut through the tentacles in a straight line just above the eyes. Discard the matter from the eyes down. Squeeze off the tiny beak at the base of the tentacles. Remove the plasticlike bone from the sac. Peel off the mottled outer skin. Wash the cleaned tentacles and sac very well.

Place the shrimp, half the olive oil, garlic, parsley, bread crumbs, and salt and pepper in a bowl. Toss well.

Stuff the squid with the shrimp mixture. Fill the sacs by three quarters and close the openings by skewering them with a toothpick. Place the remaining olive oil in a skillet large enough to hold all the squid at the same time, and heat over medium-high flame. When the oil is hot, add the squid and the tentacles, browning them well on all sides. Add the wine, lower the heat, cover the pan, and allow to simmer for 1 hour, turning the squid periodically.

Remove the squid from the pan, pull out the toothpicks, cut the sacs into three thick slices, pour the pan juices on top, and serve.

Serves 8

Cozze colle Salsicce

Mussels with Sausage

On the surface of it, this sounds like a funny combination, but I assure you that when I make this recipe people are bowled over by it. You can serve this dish like a soup, either for a first course or a main course. Omitting the bread, it can also double as a sauce for pasta.

A word about mussels: When shopping for mussels, take extra time, if necessary, to seek out cultivated mussels. They are grown on big barrels or drums in selected spots in the cleanest, most aerated water off places like Prince Edward Island in Nova Scotia. In other words, cultivated doesn't mean they were raised indoors somewhere on a "mussel farm." Cultivated mussels are very clean, with no sand or grit, full, plump, and juicy; they taste every bit as good as the "wild" ones. What's more, they don't have the beard, which can be a pain in the neck to pull off, especially if you're cooking multiple dozens of them. (If you do buy regular mussels, simply grab the beard firmly and pull it off.)

⅓ **cup extra-virgin olive oil**

3 **medium onions, peeled and cut into ¼-inch dice**

3 **large cloves garlic, peeled and crushed**

Generous pinch of crushed red pepper flakes

4 **ounces thinly sliced prosciutto, finely diced**

1 **pound sweet Italian sausage, removed from the casings and broken into small pieces**

4 **large tomatoes, peeled, seeded, and diced (if fresh are not available, use one 28-ounce can, drained and diced)**

1 **bay leaf**

⅔ **cup dry white wine**

4 **pounds mussels, cleaned and washed well (discard any whose shells don't stay closed)**

¼ **cup fresh Italian parsley, finely chopped**

6 **thick slices Italian bread, brushed with olive oil and toasted**

Place the olive oil in a sauce pot large enough to hold all the ingredients and heat over medium heat. Sauté the onions and garlic for 3 to 4 minutes or until transparent. Add the red pepper flakes, prosciutto, and sausage meat, cooking just until the meat loses its red color. Add the tomatoes and bay leaf, mix well, and allow to simmer for 5 minutes. Add the wine and allow the mixture to come to a boil. Add the mussels and parsley, cover the pot, and cook just until the mussels open, about 4 minutes. Do not overcook. Discard any mussels that do not open.

Serve the dish in deep soup bowls. Place a slice of the Italian bread on the bottom, spoon the mussels, sausage, and broth on top, and serve immediately.

Serves 6

I Pescatori

FISHERMEN IN THE BAY OF NAPLES

In the Bay of Naples, fishermen ply their trade each day, as they have for thousands of years. Out of ports like Sorrento, they have the big fishing trawlers with motor-driven nets, employing modern efficiency to bring the freshest seafood to market. The guys I love, though, are the old-timers, who you'll find around the smaller marinas and bays—guys with names like Pasquale, Ignazio, and Aniello in their mid- to late seventies who've been fishing since they were fifteen or sixteen. It's a hard life. They've seen a lot of fish but not a lot of money. Spend some time with them and they'll show you their old-fashioned ways and tell you their stories.

Like fishermen everywhere, they have their superstitions. On a recent trip, we talked to Ignazio Romano, a native of Marina di Puolo. Along with his associate, Aniello di Leva, he employs the traditional fishing technique, guiding his rowboat in a tight circle while laying down his net, then hauling it in with a wide variety of little fish. He explained an old saying—*Aferre fa bene, o forrone fa male* (The white dolphin does good, the black one bad). Legend has it that the white dolphin (*delfina bianca*, or *aferre*, in Neapolitan dialect) is a benevolent creature who looks after fishermen and will save a human being who's in trouble in the water. The black dolphin, on the other hand, is trouble. He breaks nets, steals fish from the fishermen, and brings bad luck.

One of my fondest memories of these traditional fishermen is the way they go out after octopus. I thought the Sicilian *tonnara*, where they "harpoon" the big tuna just off shore, was outrageous. Then I saw the octopus fishermen in the Bay of Naples. They row their little boats out into the bay and lower their traps, which are clay pots on the end of ropes. When the octopuses, which can grow as large as ten kilos (twenty-two pounds), crawl into those pots to hide, the fisherman haul them on board and bite them right between the eyes, otherwise they'll squirm away and slither right back into the water. How do I know about all this? I went out on the boats with the fishermen and watched them do it. I didn't believe it either until I saw it.

Like squid, octopus must be cooked either very briefly in a pan or on a grill, or braised over low heat for a very long time. There are no in-betweens. But first octopus needs to be blanched for about 2 or 3 minutes in boiling water with a little vinegar. This loosens up the purplish outer skin, which can be rubbed off. My favorite way of cooking it is on the grill. Simply marinate it with some lemon juice, olive oil, white wine, chopped fresh herbs such as marjoram or oregano, and a touch of minced garlic.

In the Bay of Naples, there is an abundance of fish, some of them familiar to East Coast (American) natives, others strictly indigenous to the Mediterranean. Many of them are small and tough to eat because they don't have a lot of flesh, but they can provide tremendous flavor and substance for broths and soups. Among them are *merluzzo*, whiting, a smaller member of the cod family; *cernia*, tilefish; *scorfano*, rock-fish, a redfish that looks like a small grouper; *dentice*, pink porgy; *orate*, dory (*dorade* in French), which is similar to what we call porgy; *spigola*, striped bass; *alici*, anchovies but bigger than the canned kind we know; *sgombri*, mack-erel; *triglia*, a type of mullet with yellow stripes; *taccone*, like a small flounder; *lucerna*, a type of dogfish or small big-headed member of the shark family; and the list goes on. . . .

There are also several kinds of squid. *Calamari* are the kind we're familiar with and that are becoming more and more common in America with the increasing popularity of different ethnic cuisines. They often come in baby size—tender, succulent, and only a couple inches long. *Totonni* are summer squid or flying squid, a bigger version of *calamari*. *Seppie* ("cuttlefish") are like larger squid and grow to be sixteen inches in length and have ten tentacles. *Seppie* are cooked in their own purplish-black ink and used primarily to make pasta sauce or served on their own in a famous dish called Seppie a la Veneziana ("Venetian style"). There are also the shellfish: *aragosta*, a Mediterranean lobster with small claws; *gam-beri*, shrimp, and *scampi*, a type of prawn that has very sweet, tender meat.

Fritto Misto di Mare

Assorted Fried Seafood

Fritto misto in one form or another is found in just about any culture that is oriented to the sea. I associate it particularly with Naples and the surrounding towns. It should show off the best of fresh local seafood.

In this recipe, I suggest using smelt, a smallish white-fleshed fish with high fat content, like a big sardine. Whitebait is another possibility, a smaller fish with shiny scales and a bright silver stripe down its side. If you've ever been deep-sea fishing off the northeastern U.S. coast, this is the most commonly used bait, a bite-size snack for a big tuna, swordfish, or shark. Of course, it's also perfectly good for humans to eat whole. Cuttlefish, known as *seppia* in Italy, is like a large squid with a few extra tentacles. It's popular in both the Mediterranean and Asia, so if the Italian markets don't have it, try the Chinese, Korean, or Thai markets. You can play around with all kinds of additions to this recipe in terms of the "assorted seafood," including clams, oysters, mussels, shrimp, and, of course, all your favorite kinds of gilled fish. I like to limit the numbers to three or four, but if you're entertaining a platoon for dinner, be expansive.

2 cups all-purpose flour

Salt and freshly ground black pepper to taste

1 cup milk

Canola or other light vegetable oil for frying

½ pound smelts or whitebait, cleaned

¾ pound squid or cuttlefish, cleaned and cut into 1-inch rings

¼ pound medium-to-large shrimp, peeled and deveined

Large bunch arugula, cleaned, dried, and trimmed of tough stems, for garnish

2 lemons, cut into wedges

Place the flour in a bowl, season with salt and pepper, and mix well. Pour the milk into a separate bowl. Place the oil in a heavy-bottomed pot to a depth of about 3 inches, over medium-high flame, and heat thoroughly. Dip each piece of seafood in the milk, then dredge it in the flour, shaking off any excess. Fry the seafood in small batches in the oil until crisp and golden brown. Drain well on paper towel, sprinkle lightly with salt, place on a platter garnished with the arugula and lemon wedges. Serve immediately.

Serves 4

Gamberi e Patate alla Napolitana

Baked Shrimp, Potatoes, and Tomatoes

This casserole is as delicious as it is simple and easy to make. You can have a little fun with it at home by substituting other types of seafood such as lobster or even fillet of sole for the shrimp. Any way you make it, you're going to love it!

It is traditionally served around Christmas. I recall my grandmother served it one Christmas Eve when I was about nine years old and I had a canary named Lillo. He escaped from his cage and flew into the Christmas tree. After repeated attempts to coax Lillo back where he belonged, the decision was made to leave him alone. His food and water were in his cage; the door was open. He would go back when he was hungry. Yeah, sure! I waited for three days, and Lillo was still living in the Christmas tree. Then came Christmas Eve. My Uncle Ralph arrived. Like many Italian men, Ralph thought he was an opera singer. After a few glasses of homemade wine, Ralph decided to sing his rendition of "O Sole Mio." By his third bar, the dog ran down to the basement with his tail between his legs. By the fifth bar, Lillo came torpedoing out of the tree directly back to his cage. After that, I never closed the door again!

2 pounds medium shrimp, peeled and deveined

Coarse salt

Juice of 1 lemon

2 pounds russet potatoes, peeled

1 cup canola or other light vegetable oil for frying

Salt and freshly ground pepper to taste

2 pounds ripe plum tomatoes, thinly sliced

Pinch of crushed red pepper flakes

20 fresh basil leaves

¼ cup extra-virgin olive oil

Soak the cleaned shrimp in a bowl of ice water with salt and lemon juice for 30 minutes.

Slice the potatoes ¼ inch thick, wash them under cold running water, and dry well. Heat the canola oil in a deep skillet over medium-high heat. Fry the potatoes until golden on both sides, about 4 minutes per side. Remove the potatoes and drain on paper towels.

Preheat the oven to 375°F.

Oil the bottom of a casserole. Arrange half the potatoes in a single layer on the bottom, seasoning them with salt and pepper. Layer half the tomatoes on top of the potatoes, seasoning with salt, pepper, and red pepper flakes. Layer half the basil leaves on top of the tomatoes.

Drain the shrimp, rinse them under cold water, and arrange them in a layer on top of the basil leaves. Season the shrimp with salt and pepper and drizzle with 2 tablespoons of the olive oil. Top them with a layer of the remaining basil leaves, a layer of the remaining potatoes and finally a layer of the remaining tomatoes, seasoning each layer with salt and pepper as you go. Top the casserole with the remaining olive oil, bake in the oven for 35 minutes, and serve. The potatoes will be browned and crispy on top.

Serves 8

Maltagliati con Calamari

Squid Sautéed with Pasta and Radicchio

The name of this dish comes from its irregular-shaped homemade pasta called *maltagliati*, which means "badly cut." The maltagliati are roughly square-shaped and are usually cut with a fluted pastry cutter that gives them a wavy edge. It is a peasant dish that highlights the abundance of wonderful, sweet baby squid in the Naples area. When you prepare this dish at home, the most important thing to remember is to not overcook the calamari. Squid is famous for coming out tender if you cook it for just a very short period of time *or* if you subject it to a long, slow braising process. Otherwise—in between—it can become tough.

For the pasta

1½ cups all-purpose flour

½ cup fresh bread crumbs

4 large eggs

Salt and freshly ground black pepper
    to taste

1 tablespoon chopped fresh parsley

For the sauce

3½ tablespoons extra-virgin olive oil

2 cloves garlic, peeled and crushed

¾ pound baby squid, cleaned and cut
    into thirds (see Note)

¼ cup dry white wine

1 head radicchio, core removed, julienned

2 scallions, green and white parts, thinly
    sliced

Salt and freshly ground black pepper
    to taste

TO PREPARE THE PASTA: Mix the flour and bread crumbs together in a bowl. Form a mound with a well in the center, placing the eggs, salt, pepper, and parsley in the well. Using a wooden spoon, combine the flour and other ingredients until a dough is formed. Wrap the pasta dough in plastic and allow to rest for 30 minutes. Roll the dough out with a rolling pin until it is very thin, about ⅛ of an inch thick. Cut the dough into ½-inch squares using a fluted pastry wheel. Cook the squares in salted water until they float, about 3 minutes. Drain well, reserving ¼ cup of the cooking liquid.

TO PREPARE THE SAUCE: Place the olive oil and garlic in a skillet over medium heat and cook for 1 minute. Add the squid and cook for 2 more minutes, then deglaze with the wine. Add the radicchio, scallions, salt, and pepper and cook for 2 to 3 minutes more. Add the reserved cooking liquid and the other ingredients, tossing it all with the drained pasta. Serve immediately.

Serves 6

Note: I would define baby squid as about 2½ inches long; if you can't find them, it's not the end of the world, just substitute regular-size (about 4½- to 5-inch) squid.

Dentice con Galetti

Roasted Snapper with Chanterelles

Two ingredients not widely known for being Italian, are prepared with an Neapolitan flare.

1 red snapper, 3 pounds, scaled, gutted, rinsed well, and patted dry

Salt and freshly ground black pepper to taste

¼ cup all-purpose flour

¼ cup extra-virgin olive oil

2 leeks, washed well and thinly sliced

1 pound Idaho potatoes, peeled and cubed

1 tablespoon fresh marjoram, minced

¾ pound chanterelles or small white mushrooms

Preheat the oven to 400°F.

Season the fish inside and out with salt and pepper. Dredge the fish in flour, shaking off the excess. Place in a baking dish large enough to hold it with the vegetables and drizzle with 2 tablespoons olive oil. Bake for 15 minutes.

Meanwhile, in a skillet over medium heat, place the remaining olive oil, the leeks, and potatoes, and sauté for 10 minutes or until the potatoes are golden and the leeks are wilted. Add the chanterelles and half the marjoram and cook for 5 more minutes, stirring periodically.

Remove the baking dish from the oven and spoon the vegetables around the fish. Sprinkle with the remaining marjoram and cover the dish with aluminum foil. Raise the heat to 450°F. and bake for 15 more minutes. Uncover and serve immediately.

Serves 6

Pesce al Cartoccio

Fish in a Paper Bag

I love gimmicks in cooking, especially when they work. This is a great way to cook fish. It's guaranteed to capture the flavor and keep the fish moist. It is also tremendous fun to present your guests with a paper bag carrying a delicious surprise. This method is widely used in Italy with poultry as well as fish.

1 plain brown paper bag, the kind you get at the supermarket

4 tablespoons extra-virgin olive oil

1 whole sea bass or red snapper, about 3½ pounds, gutted and scaled

Salt and freshly ground black pepper to taste

1 tablespoon fresh rosemary leaves

3 cloves garlic, peeled and sliced

4 lemon wedges

Preheat the oven to 375°F.

Brush the bag liberally inside and out with the olive oil.

Wash the fish well inside and out, then pat dry with paper towels. Season the fish with salt and pepper inside and out. Sprinkle the fish with rosemary and garlic inside and out, then put it in the bag and close tightly. Place the bag on a baking sheet and bake it in the oven for 30 minutes. Remove from the oven and allow the fish to rest inside the bag for 3 minutes before opening. Serve with lemon wedges on the side. (Be careful that the steam doesn't burn your hand when you open the bag.)

Serves 4

Tina DiRosa's Swordfish

Tina and Luigi DiRosa graciously hosted me and my whole TV crew for a taping at their home in Brooklyn. In addition to her work as a pastry chef at Alba's in Bensonhurst, Tina is a wonderful cook. She prepared her Spaghetti Carbonara as well as one of her favorite recipes for swordfish. Now Tina is originally from Naples—she came over with her family when she was a teenager in the early sixties—and Luigi is from Sicily, so you would expect to find swordfish on their menu.

Tina starts with one-inch-thick swordfish steaks. She mixes some olive oil, salt, and pepper in one dish and some bread crumbs, salt, and parsley in another. Then she dips the fish in the oil, coats it with the bread crumbs, and bakes it in a 425°F. preheated oven for about half an hour. Meanwhile, she fries some large sliced white onions in olive oil until they're turning golden. At that point, she starts adding balsamic vinegar, a little bit at a time, until the onions start to turn brown, becoming sweet and caramelized. The whole process of cooking the onions, followed with attention and care, takes up to an hour. She adds a pinch of salt, some crushed red pepper flakes, and some ground black pepper to the onions, puts them on top of the fish, lowers the heat in the oven and bakes everything for another 15 minutes or so. Just before serving, she sprinkles some chopped fresh mint on top of the platter. The day she cooked it for us, everybody had at least two helpings. And what a beautiful dish it is!

Polenta sulla Spianatoia con Vongole

Polenta on a Board with Clams

This is a party dish, a great way to embellish the polenta—by combining it with tender sweet clams. The fun part is that once the polenta is finished, you pour it onto a pizza paddle or clean board, then bring it straight to the table. Everybody reaches out and enjoys sharing the polenta from the board. I always have trouble getting my kids to eat foods like polenta and clams, but when I serve them this way, they can't get enough. One last thing: I am a big advocate of using the instant polenta. Purists will disagree, but it cuts the cooking time by an hour, and I dare anyone to tell the difference.

> 5 pounds littleneck clams
>
> ⅓ cup extra-virgin olive oil
>
> 4 cloves garlic, peeled and finely chopped
>
> Generous pinch of crushed red pepper flakes
>
> 3 pounds ripe tomatoes, peeled, seeded, and chopped
>
> 4 cups Chicken Stock (page 216)
>
> 2 tablespoons unsalted butter
>
> 1 cup instant polenta
>
> Salt and freshly ground black pepper

Wash the clams well under cold running water, scrubbing them clean with a brush or your hands. Place the olive oil in a saucepan over medium-high heat. Sauté the garlic until it is lightly golden brown. Add the red pepper flakes and tomato. Lower the heat and allow to simmer for 5 minutes. Add the clams, cover the pan, and cook for another 5 minutes or until all the clams are opened.

As the clams are cooking, bring the chicken stock to a boil in a separate pot over medium heat. Add the butter and polenta to the pan and allow to cook for 2 minutes or until the polenta thickens. Season to taste with salt and pepper, pour it onto a clean board or pizza paddle, spooning the clams around the perimeter and the sauce on top of the polenta. (The polenta should hold the sauce on the board, particularly if you make a bit of a well in the center of it; if you like, for extra added insurance, you can use one of those carving boards with the gutter around the edge to catch the sauce.) Serve immediately.

Serves 8

Stocca alla Moda di Messina

Stocca, Messina Style

You may have heard of the Strait of Messina, a narrow body of water that separates Sicily from the mainland. In ancient Greek lore, this was the home of Scylla and Charybdis, female monsters that personified the rock and the whirlpool. Historically, Messina, on the Sicilian side of the straits, has been beset by earthquakes, including one in 1908 that wiped out the entire town. True to Sicilian tradition, though, Messina has always bounced back. It's a thriving market town and it produces some wonderful recipes, including this one for *stocca.*

I know, what the hell is *stocca?* You've heard of baccala, which is cod that has been preserved with salt. Stocca is pretty much the same thing, but no salt—air-dried codfish, formerly a poor man's food. It's not so cheap anymore, but you can get it at just about any Italian market and it's still an excellent seafood with great taste and texture. (Actually, stocca can also be dried pollock, hake, or any other member of the white-fleshed codfish family. Most of the stocca that I get is pollock.)

1 stocca fillet, 1½ pounds, soaked in cold water for 3 days, with changes of water 3 times a day (see Note)

½ cup extra-virgin olive oil

1 medium onion, peeled and thinly sliced

One 28-ounce can Italian plum tomatoes, with their juice

1½ tablespoons pine nuts

1½ tablespoons golden raisins

2 tablespoons capers, rinsed

12 Gaeta olives, pitted and coarsely chopped

2 large russet potatoes, peeled and cut into ¼-inch-thick rounds

¼ teaspoon salt

Freshly ground black pepper to taste

1 cup dry white wine

Preheat the oven to 375°F.

Split the stocca fillet in half lengthwise, remove the center bone, and cut it into medium-size chunks. Place the olive oil in a large skillet over medium-high heat and sauté the onion until wilted and golden brown, about 8 to 9 minutes. Add the tomatoes with their juice, bring to a boil, lower the heat, and allow to simmer for about 3 to 4 minutes. Add the fish, pine nuts, raisins, capers, olives, potatoes, salt, and pepper. Bring back to a simmer, add the wine, cover, and bake in the oven for 1 hour. Serve hot.

Serves 4

Note: Like its cousin baccala, stocca is very hard and dry and needs to be soaked for a long time in advance with regular changes of water. I recommend you soak it for up to 3 days but you can get away with as little as 24 hours.

Baccalaru in Guazzetto

Sicilian Codfish Stew

Baccala or salt cod . . . it used to be that many Italians or Italian-Americans wouldn't admit they ate it. It was poor man's food. That was then. Now, baccala has become chic. You can even find it on the menus of some very trendy restaurants. For me, it's still the same inexpensive, delicious dish, only nobody's ashamed to admit they eat it anymore. In the Caribbean they call it "saltfish," in Spanish it's *bacalao*, in French *morue*, and in Portugal they have about three hundred recipes for it—whatever you call it, it's salted, dried cod and the southern Italians have some of the most appealing ways of preparing it.

    2 pounds baccala
    1½ cups all-purpose flour for dredging
    ¼ cup extra-virgin olive oil
    3 cloves garlic, peeled and crushed
    1½ pounds plum tomatoes, peeled, seeded,
        and diced
    ¼ cup Chicken Stock (page 216)
    ¼ cup fresh Italian parsley, chopped
    2 tablespoons tiny golden raisins
    2 tablespoons pine nuts, toasted
    Salt and freshly ground black pepper

Soak the baccala in cold water for 3 days, changing the water no fewer than 3 times per day. Drain the baccala, pat it dry, and cut into 3-inch pieces. Dredge them in the flour, shaking off any excess. Heat the olive oil in a heavy-bottomed skillet over medium-high heat. Fry the baccala pieces in the oil until golden brown on one side.

Gently turn them and fry until brown on the other side. Remove the pieces from the pan and drain them on a plate with paper towels.

Place the garlic in the same skillet, lower the heat to medium, and sauté until golden brown. Add the tomatoes, chicken stock, parsley, raisins, pine nuts, salt, and pepper, and mix well. Lower the heat and allow to simmer for 15 minutes. Return the baccala to the skillet and allow it to simmer for an additional 15 minutes. Serve the baccala piping hot with some good crusty Italian bread on the side to mop up.

Serves 6

La Tonnara

AN ANCIENT RITUAL

Sicily can boast one of the world's greatest fishing traditions: the ancient ritual of the *tonnara*. *Tonno* is the word for tuna and the tonnara is Sicily's equivalent to the old New England whaling tradition, only it goes back a lot further.

I remember witnessing the tonnara, truly an amazing sight, on visits to Castellammare as a young boy. For anybody used to fishing on the East Coast of America, it is just outrageous. The tonnara owes its existence to certain unique conditions. In Castellammare and other nearby fishing towns, there's a steep underwater shelf just outside the harbor. Any fisherman knows what that means: deep-sea fishing right off-shore. The tuna move from east to west as part of their annual spawning migration, making their appearances predictably in late spring and early summer.

We would watch the tonnara right from the jetty on the harbor of Castellammare. Between mid-April and late June, the fishermen lay down their nets, which are arrayed in a series of chambers specially designed to trap the big tuna. The main trap is called the "killing room" *(camera della morte)*. Once it is full of big fish, the order goes out to man the boats and begin the *mattanza*, or *occisa* ("killing"). Teams of thirty-five to forty men from the town take to their old wooden boats, which can be up to sixty feet long. I remember that they all rowed standing up and singing sea chanteys. They position the boats around the nets, banging on the sides of them with their oars and raising a terrible racket. Then they pull up the nets, gaff the tuna, and haul them right onto the boats. You've got to be strong to haul a two-hundred-pound tuna onto a big rowboat and that's exactly what these guys do. I didn't believe it until I saw it with my own eyes. They throw the big fish into the boats and right away cut off their tails to bleed them. This subdues the fish and they eventually die. Believe me, you don't want a two-hundred-pound tuna thrashing around. It's going to chew up the boat and the fishermen, too.

Involtini di Pesce Spada

Swordfish Brochettes

As I mentioned, the big oceangoing fish—tuna and sword—play a leading role in Sicilian seafood cuisine. Any major open-air food market in Sicily is going to have fish stands, and the best of them all feature beautiful chunks of swordfish. At the Vucciria in the center of Palermo, they often stand the heads up. With their big black eyes and long swords, they make an impressive display announcing loud and clear that there's fresh fish for sale.

You can broil or grill fresh swordfish and serve it with a simple dressing of lemon and/or butter. Or you can dress it up a little fancy. Here is a really clever and delicious way to dress it up.

Special equipment: You will need 1 dozen bamboo skewers along with a grill brush to apply the olive oil and sauce. Soak bamboo skewers in water first so they don't burn. You can also use metal skewers.

3 pounds swordfish steaks, ¾ inches thick, skin removed

For the stuffing

6 tablespoons extra-virgin olive oil

¼ medium white onion, peeled and chopped

2 cloves garlic, peeled and crushed

Pinch of crushed red pepper flakes

2 cups fresh bread crumbs

4 tablespoons capers, rinsed and coarsely chopped

5 tablespoons freshly grated pecorino romano cheese

1 teaspoon freshly grated lemon zest

1 teaspoon chopped fresh Italian parsley

Salt and freshly ground black pepper

Juice of 1 lemon

For the assembly

15 bay leaves, cut in half

6 scallions, green and white parts, cut into 1-inch segments

Extra-virgin olive oil for brushing

12 bamboo skewers, soaked in water

For the sauce

⅓ cup extra-virgin olive oil

2½ tablespoons freshly squeezed lemon juice

1 teaspoon freshly grated lemon zest

½ teaspoon fresh oregano leaves

¾ teaspoon salt

½ teaspoon freshly ground black pepper

¼ teaspoon granulated sugar

1 tablespoon chopped fresh Italian parsley

Cut the swordfish into twenty-four 3-inch squares. Pound each square thin. Chop any scraps of fish and reserve for the stuffing. Keep the squares refrigerated.

TO PREPARE THE STUFFING: Heat the olive oil in a skillet over medium heat. Add the scraps of swordfish, onion, garlic, and red pepper flakes and sauté for 2 to 3 minutes. Add the bread crumbs and cook for about 1 minute. Remove the contents of the skillet to a mixing bowl and add the remaining ingredients for the stuffing. Mix well, adding 1 tablespoon of water to help the mixture bind together.

Lay the swordfish squares out on a board and place an equal amount of stuffing in the middle of each square. Roll up each square.

Slide a piece of bay leaf onto a bamboo skewer, then a piece of scallion, a swordfish brochette, another piece of scallion, and a bay leaf. Repeat the procedure for each skewer so that you have 2 swordfish brochettes per skewer. Brush each skewer with olive oil and refrigerate until ready to grill.

TO PREPARE THE SAUCE: Place the olive oil, lemon juice, lemon zest, oregano, salt, pepper, and sugar, along with 2 tablespoons of water, in a blender and blend till smooth. Stir in the parsley after blending. Grill the skewers of swordfish 1 minute per side either on your barbecue or in the broiler. (Alternatively, they can be sautéed in a pan with some olive oil to prevent sticking, also 1 minute per side.) Brush the brochettes with the sauce and serve immediately with a salad on the side.

Serves 6

(with 4 brochettes per person)

Sgombro alla Griglia

Grilled Mackerel

When I was a kid, we used to go fishing for mackerel off the party boats out of Sheepshead Bay, Brooklyn. It was a half day of fishing for ten dollars and we used to come back with burlap bags full of mackerel. The only problem was that we couldn't use them all ourselves. We tried to give them away, but most people didn't want them because of the oily taste. To be honest, I was never really crazy about mackerel either, until I was shown this recipe. It's a traditional Sicilian way of grilling fish that should change your mind about mackerel, too.

3 tablespoons extra-virgin olive oil

About 1 teaspoon salt

About ¾ teaspoon freshly ground black pepper

1½ teaspoons fresh lemon juice

Four 8-ounce mackerel

1 clove garlic, peeled and chopped

1 teaspoon chopped fresh Italian parsley

1 small sprig fresh oregano, leaves only

Pinch of crushed red pepper flakes

1 tablespoon red wine vinegar

Place 1 tablespoon of the olive oil, the salt, pepper, lemon juice, and fish in a bowl. Toss well and allow to marinate for 2 hours. Grill the mackerel for 15 minutes on each side at the top of your broiler or even better on a grill, basting with the marinade as it cooks.

While the fish cooks, combine the garlic, parsley, oregano, red pepper, remaining olive oil, and vinegar. Mix well and pour over the fish when it's ready to serve.

Serves 4

Couscous di Pisci al Siciliano

Fish Couscous, Sicilian Style

You might ask, what is couscous, a traditional dish in North Africa, doing in Sicily? Well, when the Arabs conquered Sicily centuries ago, they introduced some of their culture and customs—including couscous.

Couscous is a popular dish in the western Sicilian town of Trapani, where many waterside restaurants serve their own versions with fish. The name *couscous* actually refers to the coarse grains of semolina themselves. (Semolina, by the way, is durum wheat flour, which is the same thing most high-quality pastas are made from.) It also describes the dishes made with the grains, usually including lamb or beef.

Of course, every country has its own special style of couscous. Traditional couscous is steamed for about an hour and a half and served with different meats, vegetables, and sauces on a big communal plate in the middle of the table. Nowadays, you can find precooked or "instant" couscous that can be prepared in minutes. Not many people have time for the long-cooking type and to be perfectly honest it's not much different from the precooked. (I know, it's just like polenta—the purists are going to be up in arms about this one, too. . . .)

Apart from the couscous, this recipe has a couple of other "exotic" touches, namely the ground almonds and cinnamon, that distinguish it from your everyday fish dishes.

5 pounds saltwater fish, such as snapper, tilefish, monkfish, or sea bass

Salt and freshly ground black pepper

½ cup extra-virgin olive oil

2 pounds medium squid

1 medium onion, peeled and finely chopped

¼ teaspoon ground cinnamon

1 bay leaf

1 carrot, peeled and thinly sliced

¼ teaspoon cayenne pepper

6 large tomatoes, peeled, seeded, and chopped

¾ cup fresh Italian parsley, leaves only

7 cloves garlic, peeled

For the couscous

¼ cup extra-virgin olive oil

1 small onion, peeled and finely chopped

1½ teaspoons salt

1 teaspoon freshly ground black pepper

1 teaspoon ground cinnamon

1 bay leaf

4 cups precooked couscous

12 mussels, well cleaned (see Note, page 31)

½ cup toasted blanched almonds, ground fine

3 tablespoons chopped fresh Italian parsley

Clean and bone all the fish, reserve the bones and heads, and cut the flesh into large chunks. (Have your fishmonger do this for you, if you like.) Place the chunks of fish in a bowl, season them with salt and pepper, brush with 2 tablespoons of the olive oil, cover the bowl with plastic wrap, and refrigerate.

Clean the squid by rinsing it under cold water and peeling off the dark outside skin. Pull the head from the body, cutting the tentacles below the eyes. Save the tentacles and the sac, discarding the other matter. Wash the sac and discard the viscera and quill from the inside. Cut the sac into ¼-inch-thick rings. Refrigerate the rings and cleaned tentacles until ready to use. (You can buy the squid cleaned, that is, the sacs and tentacles only, at the fish market.)

Place 6 tablespoons of the olive oil in a large casserole over medium heat and sauté the onion for 5 minutes or until soft but not browned. Add the fish heads and bones with the cinnamon, bay leaf, carrot, 1 tablespoon salt, 2 teaspoons freshly ground black pepper, and cayenne pepper and sauté for 5 minutes. Add the tomatoes with ½ cup of water. Allow to simmer over low heat, uncovered, for 15 minutes. Pass the entire contents of the pot through a food mill, pressing to extract all the juices.

Puree the parsley, garlic, and fish stock in a blender until smooth. Place it in a saucepan with 3 cups of water over a medium heat and bring to a simmer. Add the squid and allow to simmer on low heat for 35 minutes or until tender.

TO PREPARE THE COUSCOUS: As the squid is simmering, place the ¼ cup of olive oil in a casserole, add the onion, and sauté for 4 minutes. Add the salt, pepper, cinnamon, bay leaf, and 3 cups of water. Allow to come to a boil, remove from the heat, stir in the couscous, cover, and allow to stand for 3 minutes.

Add the fish to the casserole with the squid, allowing to cook for 5 minutes. Add the mussels, cover, and cook for 2 minutes or until opened. Remove the mussels and set aside. (Discard any mussels that have not opened.) Stir in the ground almonds and adjust the seasoning.

Mound the couscous in the center of a platter, fluff it with a fork, and remove the bay leaf. Distribute the fish around the couscous and decorate the platter with the mussels. Spoon the fish sauce over the couscous (it should be wet but not too soupy). Sprinkle with the parsley and serve.

Serves 8

Insalata di Gambereddi e Finucchi

Salad of Marinated Shrimp and Fennel

Everybody loves shrimp. It's a treat for special occasions . . . a night out on the town, a holiday meal at home with the relatives. Fennel is a different story. Although it's available now in many fine supermarket produce sections, many Americans consider it a curiosity. They don't know quite what to do with it.

In Italy, fennel is widely consumed not only in prepared dishes, but raw either in salads or by itself after a meal. Its mild licorice flavor and wonderfully crunchy texture makes it a superb palate cleanser and aid to digestion. Just think of a perfectly fresh stalk of celery but more dense and with a refreshing flavor twist.

Wild fennel grows all over the mountains of Sicily. The plant is smaller, and the edible part is longer and thinner than that of cultivated fennel. It doesn't have such big, plump bulbs, and it has many more thin greens growing off it. It also has a stronger, more pronounced licorice-type flavor, which is why it is often used in this dried, more mellow form. They call it *finochietto selvaggio della montagna* ("little wild mountain fennel").

You're probably familiar with the traditional Italian seafood salad dressed with lemon and olive oil. This is something different, with an excitingly tangy dressing—a more complex preparation, but well worth the effort. The flavors of fennel and shrimp—both distinctive yet subtle—marry extremely well.

You can also use lobster or crab.

2 large fennel heads, tops trimmed off

¾ cup dry white wine

1 cup Chicken Stock (page 216)

4 tablespoons extra-virgin olive oil

2 lemons

2 sprigs fresh thyme

1 bay leaf

1 teaspoon salt

8 whole black peppercorns

1 celery stalk

2 pounds medium shrimp (U-15, which is 15 shrimp or fewer to the pound; see page 117), peeled and deveined

For the salsa verde

½ cup chopped fresh Italian parsley

3 anchovy fillets, chopped

½ red onion, finely chopped, squeezed of excess juice in a paper towel

2 tablespoons capers, rinsed

2 cloves garlic, peeled and chopped

¼ cup freshly squeezed lemon juice

¾ cup extra-virgin olive oil

Salt and freshly ground black pepper

Trim the top and any bruised spots off the fennel. Slice the fennel lengthwise ½ inch thick. Place in a large nonaluminum saucepan (see Note) with the wine, stock, olive oil, juice of 1 lemon, thyme, bay leaf, salt, and peppercorns. Bring the liquid to a boil over medium heat and allow to simmer for 15 minutes or until the fennel is tender. Remove the fennel and continue to cook the liquid until it's reduced to ¼ cup, then pour it over the fennel and allow to cool.

Place the juice of the second lemon in a nonaluminum saucepan along with the celery and enough water to cover all the shrimp. Bring the water to a boil over medium-high heat, drop the shrimp in, allow the water to come back to a boil, count to thirty, then remove the shrimp from the pot and allow them to cool.

TO PREPARE THE SALSA: Combine the parsley, anchovies, onion, capers, garlic, and lemon juice in a bowl large enough to hold all the fennel and shrimp. Whisk in the olive oil and season to taste with salt and pepper. Add the fennel and shrimp to the bowl, toss well, and allow to marinate at room temperature for at least 1 hour before serving.

Serves 8

Note: Never cook anything with an acidic content—for example, vinegar, or lemon juice—in an aluminum vessel. The acid will react with the aluminum, turning the food a darker color and actually adding traces of aluminum to your food. By the same token, I'm not crazy about using cast iron for cooking dishes that have liquid. There's nothing better than cast iron for cooking a steak, but when it comes to this type of dish, always use stainless steel or ceramic.

Le "Femminelle"

She-Crabs Marinara

This is a Sicilian favorite on Christmas Eve, which is traditionally a meatless meal. Although the recipe calls for she-crabs—thus the intriguing name—you can substitute any hard- or soft-shell crab.

6 tablespoons extra-virgin olive oil

4 cloves garlic, peeled and chopped

Pinch of crushed red pepper flakes

2¼ pounds ripe plum tomatoes, peeled, seeded, and chopped

¼ cup Chicken Stock (page 216)

Salt and freshly ground black pepper

10 sprigs fresh Italian parsley, leaves only, chopped

12 crabs, about 3 pounds, cleaned (see Note)

Place the olive oil in a sauce pot large enough to hold all the crabs over medium heat. Sauté the garlic with the red pepper flakes for 2 minutes or until the garlic begins to turn golden. Add the tomatoes and chicken stock, season with salt and pepper, lower the heat, and simmer for 15 minutes. If the sauce gets too thick, add a little water. Add the parsley and crabs and allow them to simmer for an additional 15 minutes. Adjust the seasonings and serve.

Serves 6

Note: To clean the crabs, turn them over, and remove the apron or flap by pulling it off. Grab the points on the top of the shell with your left hand, grab the bottom legs in your right hand, and separate the top of the shell from the bottom. Remove the feathery gills from inside and the crabs are ready to eat. (If you want to save yourself the trouble, have them cleaned at the market.)

A Word About Shrimp

Shrimp are sized by how many there are to a pound. Jumbo shrimp are normally U-8, which is 8 or less to a pound but they can be as big as U-4; medium-size are about U-15 and small are U-18 to U-20. The larger the shrimp, the more expensive they are, so if you want to save a little money on a recipe that calls for medium size, you might go down a size and buy U-20.

The gigantic, "monster" shrimp (U-4s or 6s) are suitable for grilling, for entrées, and also for shrimp cocktail. Medium-size U-15s to U-20s work well for salads and stews. The little guys, U-28 to U-36, are great for pasta dishes, risottos, and soups. Whatever size shrimp you use, be extremely careful not to overcook them. Shrimp, called *gamberi* in standard Italian, require very little cook-ing, and if you go too far, they become tough.

Scampi in Italy are not shrimp at all but a different animal—a small crustacean, four to eight inches long, like a little lobster. They fall under one of several definitions of the word *prawn* and are found mostly in the Mediter-ranean. In France, they are called *langoustines*, which means "little lobsters." They are just heaven to eat, sweet and tender as can be.

Here's where the confusion arises: On American and Italian-American menus, there is often a dish referred to as *scampi* (or "prawns"); this is a bit of a misnomer since it is nothing more than jumbo shrimp, usually butterflied, spread with butter and/or olive oil and garlic, and grilled or broiled.

Mirruzzu al Marinaio

Whiting, Fisherman's Style

For my first public television series, I did a segment on the famous Fulton Fish Market in downtown Manhattan, the exciting hub of New York City's seafood industry. To my surprise, we discovered that the most popular fish in the market is whiting. Maybe I shouldn't have been so surprised: I ate enough of it when I was a kid. It was especially popular because of the relatively low price. The whiting's light white flesh lends itself to many preparations and this one is a highlight. Whiting is actually a smaller relative of the cod, and in Italian they both fall under the heading of *merluzzo*, which becomes *mirruzzu* in Sicilian.

6 tablespoons extra-virgin olive oil

8 anchovy fillets, packed in oil, drained

15 sprigs fresh Italian parsley, leaves only, finely chopped

1 clove garlic, peeled and finely chopped

6 whiting fillets, about 1½ pounds

Salt and freshly ground black pepper

4 sprigs fresh rosemary

2 tablespoons fresh bread crumbs

1 large lemon, cut into thin slices

Juice of 1 lemon

Preheat the oven to 400°F.

Heat 4 tablespoons of the olive oil in a saucepan over low heat. Add the anchovies, mash with a fork, and cook until just dissolved, about 30 seconds. Don't let the oil get too hot. Pour the anchovy sauce into a bowl and reserve. Mix the parsley and garlic together and set aside.

Lightly oil an ovenproof glass dish with the remaining 2 tablespoons of olive oil and lay 3 of the whiting fillets in it, skin side down. Pour some of the anchovy sauce over the fillets, season with salt and pepper, and place a sprig of rosemary on top. Place the 3 remaining fillets, skin side up, on top of the sauced ones. Pour the remaining sauce on top and sprinkle with the chopped parsley-garlic mixture. Sprinkle with the bread crumbs and season to taste with salt and pepper. Lay the lemon slices on top and finally place the remaining sprigs of rosemary on top of everything. Bake in the oven for 35 minutes.

To serve, remove the dish from the oven, discard the lemon slices, place the fish on a warm platter, squeeze the lemon juice on top, and serve.

Serves 6

Sardi a Beccaficu

Stuffed Fresh Sardines

Although they're found all over the Mediterranean, fresh sardines are foreign to most people in America. We're so used to the canned variety. Nowadays, you can find the fresh ones at your better fish markets. Sometimes you may have to ask in advance, but the fishmonger should be delighted to fill your request. Be sure to choose medium-size sardines for this recipe. And from this day on, once you've tried out this recipe, shame on you if you eat another canned sardine!

16 fresh medium sardines, about 2 pounds (there should be about 8 per pound)

½ cup plus 3 tablespoons extra-virgin olive oil

4 tablespoons fresh bread crumbs

2 tablespoons golden raisins

1 tablespoon pine nuts

½ teaspoon granulated sugar

½ teaspoon salt

Freshly ground black pepper

1 tablespoon chopped fresh Italian parsley

10 anchovy fillets, chopped

1 bay leaf, cut into quarters

Juice of 1 lemon

Scale and fillet the sardines—or ask your fish market to do it for you. Wash the fillets gently under cold water, keeping them paired.

Preheat the oven to 400°F.

To make the stuffing, combine the ½ cup of olive oil, bread crumbs, raisins, pine nuts, sugar, salt, pepper, parsley, and anchovies in a bowl, mixing well. Place a spoonful of the stuffing between each pair of fillets to form a "sandwich." Lightly oil the bottom of an ovenproof glass baking dish and lay the stuffed sardines in it. Put the bay leaf quarters on top and drizzle with the remaining olive oil. If there is any stuffing left, sprinkle it over the fish. Bake for 20 minutes. Remove the dish from the oven, place the sardines on a warm platter, squeeze the lemon juice on top, and serve with something light, such as an arugula salad, on the side.

Serves 4

Pisci Arrustutu chi Finucchi

Pan-Roasted Bass with Fennel, Sicilian Style

There are a few hard-and-fast rules of cooking and here's one of them: Anything is better cooked on the bone, whether it's fish, beef, or chicken. You get better flavor and the meat turns out more moist and juicy. This recipe calls for bass, called *branzino* in Italian, but you can substitute other fish, such as small snapper. The only thing I ask is that you make absolutely sure the fish is fresh. Always remember: Anything that smells fishy, leave where you found it.

2 small sea bass or striped bass, about 1½ pounds each, scaled and gutted

2 large fennel bulbs, the tops cut off and discarded

¼ cup extra-virgin olive oil

¼ cup dry white wine

½ pound fresh firm white mushrooms, cleaned

Salt and freshly ground black pepper

Wash the fish inside and out with cold water. Slice the fennel bulbs lengthwise, about ¼ inch thick. Place the fennel slices in a sauté pan large enough to accommodate all the fish over a medium heat. Add the olive oil, white wine, mushrooms, salt, pepper, and about 1 cup of water. Cover the pan, lower the heat, and allow to cook for about 30 minutes or until the fennel is completely tender. If the fennel becomes too dry, add another ¼ cup of water.

When the fennel is tender, uncover the pan, stir, and continue to cook as the liquid evaporates. Move the fennel to one side of the pan and

FILLETING A FISH AT THE TABLE

First you need a couple of pieces of basic equipment: two large spoons or, alternatively, a large spoon and a large flat knife (or special fish-filleting knife). Lay the fish on its side on a platter. Start by gently working the spoon in a line right down the middle of the fish on a central axis, from the gills or side fins in the front to the tail in back. This action should separate the flesh of the top of the fillet into two pieces, which you then slide back out of the way to reveal the bones. Next, hold down the bottom of the fillet using one of the spoons (or the flat width of the knife if you're using a knife) in one hand. Grip the tail securely between the thumb and forefinger of the other hand and pull it up and away, separating the tail, bones, and head from the bottom.

slide the fish in. Spoon some of the cooking liquid over the fish in the pan. Cover and cook for 6 to 7 minutes. Turn the fish over and allow to cook for an additional 5 minutes. Transfer the fish to a warm platter, spoon the pan juices and fennel on top, and serve.

Serves 4

Tunnu Auruduci

Sautéed Sweet-and-Sour Tuna Steaks

Auruduci is the Sicilian way of saying *agro-dolce* or "sweet-and-sour." This is definitely not the type of sweet-and-sour dish you find in Chinese restaurants. It is a wonderful, subtle recipe that shows off the number one fish in Sicily—tuna. This could be my favorite of the many Sicilian tuna recipes I've encountered over the years. You have to make it with fresh tuna, and always remember, serve it rare—never overcook it.

    2½ pounds fresh tuna steaks, ½ inch thick
    ⅓ cup extra-virgin olive oil
    2 medium onions, peeled and thinly sliced
    Salt and freshly ground black pepper
    ¾ cup all-purpose flour
    2 teaspoons granulated sugar
    ¼ cup red wine vinegar
    ⅓ cup dry white wine
    2 tablespoons chopped fresh Italian parsley

Over medium heat, place a skillet large enough to hold all the tuna steaks in one layer. Add 2 tablespoons of the olive oil, the sliced onions, salt, and pepper to taste. Cook the onions for about 8 to 9 minutes or until they're wilted and golden brown. Remove the onions from the pan and keep them warm.

Add 2 more tablespoons of the olive oil to the same pan and increase the heat to high. Season the tuna steaks with salt and pepper and lightly flour them on both sides. Sear the tuna steaks for 2 minutes on each side, then remove them from the pan. Add the sugar, vinegar, wine, and cooked onions to the pan. Cook, uncovered, over medium heat for about 2 minutes. Add the parsley and the tuna steaks and cook for another 2 minutes. Remove the tuna to a warm platter, pour the pan juices on top, and serve.

Serves 6

carne e
pollame

Mary Lazzarino, my nonna

Meat is not an everyday staple in the southern Italian and Sicilian diets. Because of its cost and scarcity, in fact, meat dishes are generally reserved for special occasions. And within the realm of meat and fowl, you'll come across much more chicken, lamb, and pork than you will veal, which is reserved for *very* special occasions.

In the mountainous areas of Irpinia and other comparable regions throughout the south, there is a tradition of hunting for wild game—rabbits, pheasants, quail, wild boar. In this chapter, I offer a few game recipes—for quail and rabbit—because I just couldn't resist. Unless you're a hunter, these meats can be hard to come by in the United States. (There are a number of purveyors who sell through retail stores and via mail order. There's also nothing wrong with buying frozen game meats. Consult with your trusty neighborhood butcher shop or supermarket meat department regarding sources and availability.)

While Sicilians are generally more likely to eat fish, their island does offer some excellent meat and fowl recipes. Many of them incorporate the "foreign" or "exotic" influences we've touched on—sweet-and-sour sauce, for example, wild fennel or pomegranate. Others fall into the category of "home cooking" or comfort food—the meat loaf and the pot roast are good examples of this.

Another notable tradition in southern Italian cuisine, harking back to the theme of economy and frugality, is the consumption of offal or "specialty meats"—the hearts, heads, lungs, livers, kidneys, brains, feet, tongues, stomachs, and so forth. In Neapolitan cuisine, they have a couple of old-time favorites: *gnumerelli*, which are seasoned intestines roasted on a spit, and *soffritto*, a stew of heart, liver, and lungs. In this book I'm offering just a taste of them in the form of the Tripe Parmesan recipe. The bottom line is, nothing should ever go to waste. If you're going to roast the whole baby lamb, why leave out the head? If you want to be truly authentic, eat the head—all of it. For those who read my first book, you may recall the image of my grandfather doing just that, sitting proudly at the head of the table and grossing out all of us kids.

Great-grandfather Andrea Pesce with my grandmother's brother Michael

Agnello Napolitano all' Cacciatora con Patate e Pomodori

Neapolitan Lamb with Potatoes and Tomatoes

I have a very dear friend named Pete, who is Neapolitan, and this is the way he likes to cook his lamb. This is a typical Neapolitan preparation, with the tomatoes and onions, recalling its more famous cousin, Chicken Cacciatora. Lamb is more often than not cooked with garlic, but you'll note that this very fine recipe has none and suffers not a bit from its absence. (*Cacciatora*, by the way, is the feminine of "hunter." I've heard these dishes are named after the hunter's wife; sometimes they're called *cacciatore*, after the hunter himself. Either way, the point is that they're simple, rustic, hearty, and utterly delicious.)

My friend Pete is very particular about selecting lamb. He always looks for the lighter, milder, more tender meat. Aside from being a great cook, Pete is one of those people who can really charm people with his talk. He's incredibly popular and he makes friends with just about anyone. How popular is Pete? He's so popular that one time he was walking down the street with the pope and a guy who knew him turned to his friend and exclaimed, "Hey, who's that guy with Pete?"

3 pounds lamb ribs and back, cut into ½-inch chunks

1 large onion, peeled and thinly sliced

1 pound ripe plum tomatoes, cut into thick wedges

1 pound potatoes, peeled and cut into wedges

½ cup extra-virgin olive oil

3 sprigs fresh oregano, leaves only, chopped

3 sprigs fresh thyme, leaves only, chopped

Salt and freshly ground black pepper

Preheat the oven to 375°F.

Place the lamb in a deep roasting pan (an earthenware one is preferable). Scatter the onion, tomatoes, and potatoes around the lamb, toss well. Drizzle everything with the olive oil, sprinkle with the herbs, and season with the salt and pepper. Cover the pan and place in the oven for 1 hour. After 1 hour, uncover and roast for 10 more minutes. The lamb should be brown and crisp on the outside. Remove the lamb to a warm platter, surround it with the vegetables, spoon the pan juices on top, and serve hot.

Serves 6

Arrosto di Vitello

Roasted Shoulder of Veal with Herbs

As I may have mentioned, I've been on a real bread crumb kick: I really love the toasty flavor and crunchy texture they add to baked dishes. Several of the recipes in this book are my adaptations of classic dishes with bread crumbs as an extra added treat. In this case, they are used to "encrust" the herb-seasoned veal, a mild-flavored meat that benefits tremendously from this treatment. The other interesting flavor angle to this dish is the marsala. Although it's from Sicily, this world-famous wine finds its way into many dishes from regional cuisines all over Italy.

2 tablespoons extra-virgin olive oil

1½ tablespoons unsalted butter

One 2½-pound piece boneless veal shoulder, rolled and tied tightly

1 small white onion, peeled and finely chopped

1 teaspoon chopped fresh rosemary leaves

4 fresh sage leaves, chopped

Salt and freshly ground black pepper

⅔ cup dry white wine

½ cup sweet marsala

¼ cup freshly ground Parmesan cheese

2 tablespoons bread crumbs, lightly toasted

Place a heavy-bottomed casserole over medium-high heat. Add the olive oil and 1 tablespoon of the butter and brown the meat on all sides. Remove the meat, set it aside, and add the onion, rosemary, and sage to the casserole. Allow the onion to brown, then return the meat to the casserole and season with salt and pepper. Add the wine and marsala, lower the heat, cover the casserole, and allow to simmer over low heat for about 1½ hours, turning the meat periodically. If the casserole starts to dry out, add a little water.

Meanwhile, preheat the oven to 500°F.

Coat the bottom of a baking sheet big enough to hold the meat with the remaining butter. Mix the cheese and bread crumbs together in a bowl. Remove the meat from the pot and coat it all over with the bread crumb mixture. Place it on the baking sheet and bake it in the oven for 5 to 6 minutes or until the crust is golden brown.

While the crust is browning, warm the cooking juices in the casserole over low heat. Slice the meat thinly, arrange on a warm platter, spoon the cooking juices on top, and serve.

Serves 6

Lamb

ABBACHIO, AGNELLO, AND SO FORTH

For those of you who think a lamb is a lamb is a lamb, it's important to distinguish among a milk-fed baby lamb, a spring lamb, and a "regular" lamb. The baby is six to eight weeks old, weighs about sixteen pounds, and is generally roasted whole. A spring lamb is four to five months old; anything less than a year old is just regular lamb. *Abbachio* (ah-*bahk*-yoh) refers to the milk-fed baby lamb, which should be served well cooked; if it's medium-rare or rare, it has an unappealing mushy consistency. *Agnello* (ah-*nye*-loh) refers either to spring or regular lamb, which yields the familiar roast leg of lamb, weighing about eight pounds. The younger the lamb, the more tender the meat and the milder the flavor, which is significant to many people who don't necessarily like a strong "lamby" flavor.

In Neapolitan, they call a baby lamb a *capretto*, which in standard Italian also means "baby goat or kid." The *agnello* is a *piechoro*, related to the standard word for sheep, *pecora*. Don't ever refer to a person as a *piechoro*—that's another cup of tea. It means cuckold, and it's one of the biggest insults to an Italian. (Holding up your index finger and pinkie in someone's direction indicates the horns, and it is the equivalent of giving that person "the finger.")

Bistecca alla Pizzaiola

Steak Pizzaiola

This classic Neapolitan dish is one of my father's favorites. Now, my father is a very tough man who never likes to admit when he's wrong, but he also has a dry sense of humor. He was never very good at fixing things around the house. One day, the doorbell broke and my father decided to fix it. The only problem was he wired it wrong and it rang continuously until you pushed the button. No one dared say anything. Later, we sat down to eat and nobody uttered a word. Finally, the bell stopped ringing and my father yelled out, "Somebody getta the door!" Anyway, I remember we were eating steak pizzaiola that night.

Bottom round is a sinewy, tough, and very tasty cut of beef. After pounding it to tenderize it, this is probably the best way to dress it up—with garlic, olive oil, tomatoes, oregano, the foundations of Neapolitan cuisine and also the basis for pizza, which is why they call this dish *pizzaiola* ("pizza style").

2 pounds bottom round beef, sliced about ⅛ inch thick

Salt and freshly ground black pepper

¼ cup extra-virgin olive oil

1 medium onion, peeled and thinly sliced

2 cloves garlic, peeled and chopped

6 Italian plum tomatoes, peeled, seeded, and diced

½ cup dry red wine

2 sprigs fresh oregano

Place the meat between two pieces of wax paper and pound it very thin using a meat pounder or the bottom of a heavy skillet. Season the meat with salt and pepper. Place the olive oil in a skillet over high heat and brown the beef on both sides, then remove it and keep warm by placing it in a dish, covered with foil, on top of the warm stove. Meanwhile, lower the heat to medium, add the onion and garlic to the same pan and cook for 3 minutes or until golden brown. Add the tomatoes, wine, and salt and pepper to taste. Lower the heat and allow to simmer for 15 minutes. Pick the oregano leaves from the stem, then add them to the pan along with the steaks. Allow to cook for an additional 10 minutes and serve immediately.

Serves 6

Bracciole di Maiale

Stuffed Pork Roll

Every family has its recipe for *bracciole*. In my first book, I gave you a smaller, more common version—for beef bracciole. Here is a larger one, for pork, that does very well cooked in a tomato sauce. In my family, we used to joke about how my grandmother never, ever wasted anything. I always loved the one about how after she used the string to tie the bracciole, she'd give it to us for dental floss.

Pork loin is not at all fatty despite the pig's reputation for being a fat animal. Actually, it's one of the leaner, tastier meats and has become a very popular cut with people who want to watch their fat intake but still enjoy the occasional meat dish.

One 2½-pound boneless pork loin

Salt and freshly ground black pepper

2 cloves garlic, peeled and chopped

Five ¼-inch-thick slices mild provolone cheese (about 8 ounces), cut into medium dice

1½ tablespoons freshly grated pecorino romano cheese

1 small onion, peeled and chopped

3 sprigs fresh Italian parsley, thick stems removed

4 fresh basil leaves

2 sweet Italian sausages, removed from the casings, broken into pieces, and sautéed until lightly browned

1 hard-boiled egg, peeled and cut into quarters

2 tablespoons pure olive oil

1 recipe Ragù (page 60) (see Note)

Cut a deep slit down the center of the pork loin and open it so it lays flat. (This is the procedure known as butterflying.) Season the meat with salt and pepper to taste. Mix all the remaining ingredients, except the olive oil and gravy, well in a bowl. Lay the mixture evenly down the center of the meat. Roll the meat up tightly, tying it with butcher's twine at 1-inch intervals. Secure the ends with toothpicks.

Place the olive oil in a skillet over medium-high heat. Brown the pork roll all over, then simmer it, submerged in the gravy, over very low heat until tender, 1 to 1½ hours. (Alternatively, the bracciole can be roasted in the oven and topped with gravy when done.)

When it's done, remove the bracciole to a cutting board, cut off the twine, pull out and discard the toothpicks. Slice the bracciole into ½-inch-thick slices, place on a warm platter, and serve with the gravy.

Serves 8

Note: I am not going to recommend that you take any shortcuts and simply use your favorite tomato sauce here. It's possible, but the authentic Famous Sunday Gravy is definitely going to yield the best results. Now you know how I feel; it's your choice.

Fagioli dall'Occhio con Luganega

Luganega Sausage with Black-eyed Peas

Yes, America, we also eat black-eyed peas in Italy. In fact, we love them—at least I do. In this recipe, I pair them with my favorite type of sausage, which is called luganega and is commonly known as a "pinwheel" or a "cheese-and-parsley ring." It's much thinner in diameter than your standard Italian sausage and it comes coiled up in a spiral shape with four wooden brochettes holding it together. You can find it in any Italian deli, usually made with cheese and parsley. Nowadays there are all kinds, including chicken, fennel, sun-dried tomatoes, spinach—you name it.

Luganega is easy to barbecue and takes much less time on the grill than standard sausage. If, for some reason, you can't find it, simply substitute regular Italian sausage. This recipe is a meal in itself. Another reason I love it is because it works very well if you prepare it in advance and reheat it. Now you don't have any excuse not to try it.

¼ cup extra-virgin olive oil

1 small onion, peeled and finely chopped

3 cloves garlic, peeled and finely chopped

⅓ cup finely diced carrot

⅓ cup finely diced celery

5 Italian plum tomatoes, peeled and chopped

1 pound luganega sausage, cut into 2-inch lengths (see Note, page 58)

1 cup dried black-eyed peas, soaked in warm water for at least 1 hour

Salt and freshly ground black pepper

Preheat the oven to 350°F.

Place the olive oil in a heavy-bottomed casserole over medium heat. Sauté the onion until golden. Add the garlic and cook for an additional 2 minutes. Add the carrot and celery and cook, stirring, for an additional 5 minutes. Add the tomatoes, lower the heat to low, and allow to simmer for about 15 minutes.

Add the sausage and allow to simmer for an additional 10 minutes. Add the black-eyed peas along with enough water to cover them completely. Bring the liquid to a simmer, cover, and place the casserole in the oven for 1½ hours, until the black-eyed peas are completely cooked. If they become too dry, add a little more water. If they're too liquid, uncover and let some of the liquid evaporate. The dish should not be soupy, but rather the thicker consistency of a stew.

When the sausages are done, hold the handle of the pan and slide it partially off the heat. Tip it slightly so the liquids collect on one side. The fat will be bubbling on top, and while the liquid is still boiling, skim it off. Season with salt and pepper to taste, and serve.

Serves 4

Involtini di Vitello

Stuffed Bundles of Veal

When you buy the veal for this recipe, splurge a little and ask for the *scallopine* ("cutlets") from the leg, rather than the shoulder. The shoulder cut is less expensive, but tougher. The meat that is lighter in color is younger and more tender. You can substitute chicken cutlets for the veal: either way, this recipe makes for a great meal.

> **Four 4-ounce slices veal scallopine, pounded very thin, about 1/16 inch (see Note)**
>
> **2 ounces mozzarella cheese, cut into 1/4-inch dice**
>
> **2 ounces prosciutto, finely diced**
>
> **5 sprigs fresh Italian parsley, leaves only, finely chopped**
>
> **1/4 cup freshly grated Parmesan cheese**
>
> **Salt and freshly ground black pepper to taste**
>
> **1/4 cup all-purpose flour**
>
> **2 tablespoons extra-virgin olive oil**
>
> **1/2 cup dry white wine**

Lay the pounded veal cutlets flat on a board. Thoroughly mix the mozzarella, prosciutto, parsley, and Parmesan in a bowl. Place an even portion of the mixture in the center of each cutlet and season lightly with salt and pepper. Roll each cutlet up, making sure to fold over the ends to keep the mixture inside, then secure each one by tying it with string. (Most recipes call for butcher's twine; my grandmother and her friends use sewing thread, since they always have some of that around the house. You can use one length of string or thread and spiral it around a few times from one end of the *involtino* to the other.)

Roll each bundle in the flour to coat it, dusting off any excess. Place the olive oil in a skillet over high heat and cook the involtini, turning them, until golden brown on all sides. Add the wine to the pan, lower the heat to medium and cook until the wine is reduced by three quarters.

Remove the pan from the heat, cut the strings off the involtini, place them on a warm platter, pour the pan juices on top, and serve with a simple risotto or pasta dish on the side.

Serves 4

Note: You can pound the veal yourself, between two pieces of wax paper, with a meat mallet or the bottom of a skillet, but it's just as easy—and also foolproof—to have your butcher do it for you.

Petto di Tacchino Arrocchiato

Turkey Roll with Ham and Cheese

You may think of turkey as exclusively American, but it has actually been very popular in Italy for years. Italians don't generally roast the whole bird. Instead they prepare its various parts in different ways. Here is a tasty, easy, and inexpensive recipe.

1 whole turkey breast, bone removed

8 ounces pancetta, cut into strips

4 ounces boiled ham, cut into strips

1 clove garlic, peeled and thinly sliced

1 tablespoon freshly grated pecorino cheese

2 teaspoons fresh rosemary leaves

Salt and freshly ground black pepper

Preheat the oven to 400°F.

Remove the skin and butterfly the turkey breast. Open it up flat and lightly pound it. Lay the strips of pancetta and ham all over the breast, overlapping if necessary. Sprinkle with the garlic, pecorino, and 1 teaspoon of the rosemary.

Roll the breast up like a jelly roll and tie it with string. On your work surface, lay a piece of heavy-duty aluminum foil large enough to wrap around the entire turkey roll, shiny side up, and place the roll in the center. Sprinkle with the remaining rosemary and salt and pepper. Close up the aluminum foil, sealing it tight, and bake the roll in the oven for 45 minutes. Remove from the oven, allow to sit for 5 minutes, then remove the foil. Cut the strings off, slice the roll, and serve—with or without your favorite tomato sauce on top.

Serves 6

Pollo in Pane

Chicken Baked in Bread

Let me tell you something: When you taste this dish you cannot help but say "Wow!" It involves cooking an entire chicken inside a piece of bread dough as it bakes. It is a fairly complicated recipe, but like anything, it can be simplified by dividing it into stages. The stuffing is dynamite. It really enhances the flavor of the bird, while the bread seals all the flavor in. My favorite part is eating the bread, which has soaked up all the cooking juices. As I said, "Wow!" There was a cookbook published a few years back called *365 Ways to Cook Chicken*—one for each day of the year. I doubt it had anything like this.

1 chicken, about 3½ pounds

5 tablespoons extra-virgin olive oil

1 red onion, peeled and coarsely chopped

1 celery stalk, coarsely chopped

2 cloves garlic, peeled and chopped

2 carrots, peeled and coarsely chopped

5 ounces prosciutto, finely diced

**Salt and freshly ground black pepper
to taste**

½ cup dry red wine

**¼ pound chicken livers, cleaned and cut
into quarters**

**1 recipe Pane di Casa (page 218), dough only
(uncooked)**

Wash the chicken well, inside and out, then pat dry with paper towels. Place the olive oil in a large skillet over medium-high heat and sauté the onion, celery, garlic, carrots, and prosciutto for 10 minutes, stirring frequently. Remove from the pan and set aside in a bowl.

Season the chicken well, inside and out, with salt and pepper. Brown it well on all sides in the skillet, then remove to a plate to cool. Add the wine to the skillet and cook until it evaporates. Add the chicken livers and cook for 2 to 3 minutes, then remove them and allow to cool. When the livers are cool add them to the vegetable mixture in the bowl.

Roll out the bread dough on a lightly floured board to a rectangle 1 inch thick. Sprinkle the surface of the dough with salt and pepper.

Stuff the chicken with the liver mixture, then place it in the center of the dough. Fold the edges of the dough around the chicken, completely sealing in the bird and smoothing it out to a round shape. Cover the dough-encased chicken with a damp cloth and keep it in a warm place for an hour or so until it doubles in size.

Preheat the oven to 400°F.

Place the chicken-in-dough in a baking pan and bake in the oven for 60 to 70 minutes. Remove from the oven and place on a serving platter. To serve, cut off the top of the bread then remove the chicken to carve it. Serve each piece of chicken with a spoonful of the stuffing and a piece of the bread.

Serves 4

Pollo in Porchetta

Chicken, Suckling-Pig Style

Porchetta refers to a roast pig made in the traditional way, with a stuffing of herbs, spices, and pancetta. True porchetta is usually reserved for special occasions. By applying this method to chicken, even a simple dinner at home with the family becomes a special occasion.

For the stuffing
4 ounces pancetta, finely diced
10 fresh sage leaves, coarsely chopped
10 juniper berries, coarsely chopped
1 large bay leaf, coarsely chopped
1 tablespoon fresh rosemary leaves
5 whole black peppercorns
Salt and freshly ground black pepper

For the chicken
1 chicken, about 3½ pounds
¼ cup pure olive oil

TO PREPARE THE STUFFING: Mix together the pancetta, sage, juniper berries, bay leaf, rosemary, peppercorns, 2 teaspoons of salt, and ½ teaspoon of pepper. Set aside.

Preheat the oven to 425°F.

TO PREPARE THE CHICKEN: Wash the chicken well, inside and out, and pat dry. Fill the cavity of the chicken with the stuffing and sew up both ends with thread. Season the outside of the chicken liberally with salt and pepper. Place the chicken, breast side down, in a roasting pan with the olive oil. Roast the chicken for 1 hour, turning it 3 or 4 times. Remove it to a warm platter and serve immediately.

Serves 4

Polpetti

Meatballs

Who doesn't like meatballs? I did a show with Pat Cooper, the famous Italian-American comedian, during which he officially launched his quest for the best meatball in the world. He is presently searching every corner of America for the perfect meatball, so if you hear a knock on the door, you'd better have this recipe at hand. By the way, Pat's Italian name is Pasquale Caputo, so if you meet him, act like you already knew it.

One popular misconception about meatballs is that all-meat ones are better, that anybody who puts bread in them is being cheap. Wrong. The bread is what makes a meatball stay tender and prevents it from drying up. My family always uses several meats, each of which lends a different quality, but you can stick with all beef if you prefer. No substitutions for the bread, though!

3 tablespoons extra-virgin olive oil

1 small white onion, peeled and finely chopped

3 cloves garlic, peeled and chopped

1 pound ground beef

1 pound ground veal

½ pound ground pork

1¼ cup fresh bread crumbs

¾ cup freshly grated pecorino romano cheese

12 sprigs fresh Italian parsley, leaves only, chopped

8 extra-large eggs

Salt and freshly ground black pepper

MARSALA

Marsala is the delicious, world-famous fortified wine made in the town of the same name, which is at the westernmost tip of Sicily. It adds a fabulous flavor to many dishes—like Scallopine alla Marsala or the veal roast presented earlier in this chapter—and it seems to go particularly well with veal and other mildly flavored meats. Marsala is also a key ingredient in zabaglione, the whipped egg yolk dessert, the recipe for which is in my first book.

Place 1 tablespoon of the olive oil in a skillet over medium heat. Sauté the onion and garlic in it for 3 minutes or until the onion is translucent. Set aside and allow to cool. In a large bowl, mix together the three meats with the bread crumbs, cheese, the cooled onion and garlic, parsley, eggs, and salt and pepper to taste. Shape the mixture into medium-size ovals, the size of extra-large eggs. You should end up with about 22 meatballs. Brown the meatballs in 2 tablespoons of olive oil and proceed with the recipe for the Famous Sunday Gravy (Ragù, page 60) or simply submerge them in your favorite tomato sauce and gently simmer until tender.

Makes about 2 dozen meatballs

Quaglie con Ficu

Roasted Quail with Figs

In my family, we've always grown fresh figs. It's one of my favorite traditions, which I continue to uphold. I love to eat figs and I thoroughly enjoy growing them. Living on Long Island, though, with its harsh winters, always presents a challenge. A great friend of mine, Mimmo, who is Neapolitan and has a knack for growing all kinds of plants, taught me a secret for preserving a fig tree during our cold East Coast winters. In the late fall, you loosen the dirt around the base of the tree, push the tree over so it's lying on its side, and cover it with leaves and twigs. You straighten the tree out in the spring, firm up the dirt around it, and wait till the beautiful ripe figs come out in midsummer. (You can also buy them dried and/or fresh all year-round.)

Like many other fine foods common to the European table, quail has become much easier to obtain in this country over the past few years. You can buy it fresh, semi boneless, and butterflied from your local butcher or the supermarket meat section. It also should be available frozen. If not, try substituting small ducks.

1 clove garlic, peeled and chopped

3 tablespoons extra-virgin olive oil

2 teaspoons chopped fresh rosemary

2 teaspoons chopped fresh sage

8 fresh quail, butterflied, about 2½ pounds total (see Headnote)

6 dried figs, coarsely chopped

1 cup sweet marsala

3 ounces pancetta, diced

3 shallots, peeled and finely chopped

1 cup Chicken Stock (page 216)

Mix the garlic, olive oil, half the rosemary, and half the sage in a bowl, then add the quail, and toss. Allow to marinate for 30 minutes. In a separate bowl, marinate the figs in the marsala, also for 30 minutes.

Sauté the pancetta for 8 minutes in a skillet over medium-high heat until crisp. Remove the pancetta with a slotted spoon and set aside. In the same pan, sauté the quail, browning well on both sides, then set aside.

Lower the heat under the skillet and cook the shallots until softened, about 8 minutes. Raise the heat to high, add the figs and marsala, cooking until almost dry, about 6 to 7 minutes. Add the stock, reduce the heat to low, and cook until the figs are tender, about 8 minutes. Add the pancetta and remaining herbs and cook for 6 to 7 more minutes. Place the quail in the sauce for 4 minutes to heat through. Remove them to a warm platter, spoon the sauce over the top, and serve. This dish goes very well with soft polenta.

Serves 4

Trippa alla Parmigiana

Tripe Parmesan

Now tripe definitely falls into that category of foods that most people are reluctant even to try. I bet most people have turned the page already. For those of you who have read this far and are feeling a little adventurous, you are in for a treat. When prepared correctly, tripe is tender, succulent, and has tremendous flavors and aromas. This is by far the best recipe for tripe I've ever come across. In my first book, I said tripe with red beans was the best; since then, I have discovered this and I'm convinced it's even better.

Tripe is the stomach lining of a cow. There are three types of tripe because the cow has three stomach chambers. The best is honeycomb tripe, so called because it has a pattern on the inside like a honeycomb. One of the most important things to know about tripe is that you cannot overcook it. In fact, if you don't cook it long enough, it will wind up with the consistency of shoe leather. Tripe is one of those foods that's even better as a leftover; you can prepare this dish four to five days ahead of time. Just be sure to refrigerate it.

2 pounds frozen honeycomb tripe, thawed

½ cup extra-virgin olive oil

1 large onion, peeled and diced small

½ cup diced celery

½ cup diced carrots

3 cloves garlic, peeled and crushed

1 tablespoon chopped fresh Italian parsley

¼ teaspoon chopped fresh rosemary

¾ cup dry white wine

1½ cups canned tomatoes, coarsely chopped, with their juice

Salt and freshly ground black pepper

1 cup Chicken Stock (page 216)

2 tablespoons unsalted butter

¾ cup freshly grated Parmesan cheese

Rinse the tripe under cold water and place it in a sauce pot, covering it with cold water. Bring the water to a boil over high heat, lower the heat, then allow to simmer for 15 minutes. Drain the tripe, cool it under cold water, and cut it into pieces ½ inch wide and 3 inches long.

Preheat the oven to 325°F.

Place the olive oil in a heavy casserole over medium heat. Sauté the onion for 3 to 4 minutes or until golden. Add the celery and carrots and cook for another 4 minutes. Add the garlic, parsley, and rosemary and cook for another 3 minutes. Add the tripe and stir well. Then add the wine and bring to a boil, allowing it to boil for about 2 minutes. Add the tomatoes with their juice, a generous amount of pepper, salt, and the stock. Allow to come to a simmer, cover the casserole, and place it in the oven for 2½ hours. Check the casserole from time to time and if it gets too dry, add more stock. The tripe should become very tender; if not, continue to cook until it is. When the tripe is done, swirl in the butter and Parmesan and serve with rice, polenta, or potatoes on the side.

Serves 6

Pastello di Maiale Ripieno

Loin of Pork in a Crust

This is what I call a special-event recipe; that is to say that anytime you prepare this fabulous dish, it will become a special event. A roll of pork with ham, wrapped in pastry, and topped with slivered almonds: It's my own interpretation of a dish I encountered in a charming little restaurant in Sorrento. The only difference is that they used a loin of veal. I substituted pork because I find a whole loin of veal a little too pricey for the average consumer. If you want to splurge, you can simply substitute veal for the pork.

For the crust

1 teaspoon active dry yeast

¼ cup extra-virgin olive oil

½ teaspoon salt

3½ tablespoons freshly grated Parmesan cheese

1 large egg

4 cups presifted all-purpose flour

For the pork

1 boneless pork loin, about 3 pounds

12 ounces cooked ham, thinly sliced

1 tablespoon extra-virgin olive oil

1 tablespoon chopped fresh sage

½ tablespoon chopped fresh rosemary

Salt and freshly ground black pepper to taste

5 tablespoons unsalted butter, at room temperature

1 large egg, lightly beaten with 1 tablespoon water

¼ cup slivered almonds

TO PREPARE THE CRUST: Dissolve the yeast in 1 cup of warm water, then stir in 3 tablespoons of the olive oil, the salt, Parmesan, and egg. Stir in the flour a little at a time, adding just enough to make a dough that does not stick to the sides of the bowl. Place the dough on a floured surface and knead for about 5 minutes until smooth. Transfer the dough to a lightly oiled bowl, cover the bowl with a wet towel, and set aside in a warm place for about 45 minutes, allowing the dough to double in size.

Preheat the oven to 400°F.

TO PREPARE THE PORK: Using a long knife, butterfly the loin lengthwise. Lay a third of the ham slices on the loin, then roll it up crosswise into a log. Tie together with butcher's twine, place in a roasting pan, drizzle with the olive oil, sage, rosemary, salt, and pepper. Bake in the oven for 30 minutes. Remove from the oven, cut off the strings, and allow to cool.

Lower the oven temperature to 375°F.

Puree the remaining ham with the butter in a food processor to make a mousse. Roll the dough out on a floured surface to a rectangular shape ¼ inch thick and large enough to cover the pork roll. Place the cooled pork roll in the center of the dough and spread the ham-butter mousse on it, covering the whole roll. Roll the dough up around the pork roll to create a log and neatly trim off the excess in long strips. Brush the log all over with the beaten egg. Make a braid out of the dough trimmings and arrange the braid down the center of the roll on top. Brush it with beaten egg, sprinkle the roll with the almonds, and bake it in the oven for 40 minutes. Cut into slices ¾ to 1 inch thick and serve immediately.

Serves 10

Sant'Angelo dei Lombardi

Sant'Angelo, home to my maternal grandmother's side of the family, is typical of many towns in Campania and the other provinces of southern Italy in that the people are poor, almost pathetically so, but the sense of family and community is very strong. They all look out for one another. Here in America, we think we have deep roots if our family's been in the same place for most of this century. In places like Sant'Angelo, the families have roots that go back many centuries. If they're poor in a monetary sense, they're rich culturally. The recipes that have been passed down, the way they feed whole families inexpensively with one dish—many times out of one pot—reflect just one aspect of the richness and depth of the culture.

I remember when we used to visit friends and family in Sant'Angelo, and we were welcomed with open arms and shouts of joy. Sure, they were genuinely glad to see us, but they also looked to us as the wealthy relatives from America. We wouldn't dare show up without bringing gifts, which was easy because many of the things we took for granted in Brooklyn—hairpins, rubber bands, and other basic household items—were scarce over there. We would go up to the mountains for a day or two, drop in on relatives in Sant'Angelo, and enjoy long family meals in the courtyards of their little houses and apartments. And what a cast of characters would show up!

In 1980, one of the worst earthquakes ever to strike Italy devastated Avellino and the surrounding area, including Sant'Angelo. It is a testament to the spirit of its people—to their stubborn determination—that they are still rebuilding the place now, twenty years later. In the rebuilding process, they are redrawing the map of their sleepy little region of Italy, something that makes a "son of Sant'Angelo" like me proud. Sant'Angelo might very well have been a ghost town today, but it's not, thanks to its hardworking populace.

Agglassatu

Sicilian-Style Pot Roast

In Palermo, every family has its own version of this recipe. I love this one, which was demonstrated to me by my old friend Joey Baccala. Not only is Joey a great cook, but he is also a hypochondriac. When he used to go to the doctor and was told nothing was wrong, it made him very unhappy. Needless to say, he changed doctors as often as he changed his clothes. Finally, he went to the famed Sicilian doctor Dr. Vinnie Boompatz, a nut in his own right. After giving Joey a complete checkup, Dr. Vinnie told him, "I have some good news and some terrible news." Joey, who wasn't prepared to hear anything bad from a doctor, said, "Please, Doc, tell me the good news first." The doctor said, "Joey, the good news is that I am naming a disease after you."

By the way, Baccala and Boompatz are real nicknames. (I swear I didn't make them up.) Anybody who was somebody in my old neighborhood had one; if you didn't you were still nobody.

One 3-pound boneless chuck roast (have your butcher tie it for you; it makes it easier to handle)

Salt and freshly ground black pepper to taste

3 tablespoons all-purpose flour

3 tablespoons extra-virgin olive oil

2 tablespoons unsalted butter

3 pounds onions, peeled and thinly sliced

1 bay leaf

6 cloves garlic, peeled and thinly sliced

¼ teaspoon crushed red pepper flakes

2 sprigs fresh thyme

2½ cups dry white wine

1 cup sweet marsala

6½ cups Chicken Stock (page 216)

Season the roast with salt and pepper and dust it with the flour. Place the olive oil and butter in a large stockpot over medium heat and brown the roast evenly on all sides. Remove the roast to a platter and place the onions, bay leaf, garlic, red pepper flakes, and thyme in the pot. Lightly season with salt and pepper and, stirring periodically, sauté for 7 to 8 minutes or until the onions are wilted. Add the white wine and marsala, bring to a boil, and reduce the liquid by half. Add the roast back to the pot with the stock, adjust the seasonings, and allow to come back to a boil. Lower the heat, cover the pot, and allow to cook slowly for 2 hours, turning the meat every half hour, until fork tender. Remove the meat from the pot and keep it warm on a covered platter. Raise the heat, bring the sauce to a boil, and reduce by half. You should end up with a gravy that is light brown in color and the consistency of heavy cream.

Remove the string from the roast, cut the meat into thin slices, remove the thyme and bay leaf from the sauce. Spoon the sauce, including the onions, on top of the meat slices and serve.

Serves 6

The Connection

The traditional Little Italy section of Manhattan, what was once a real slice of the old country, a pulsating center of our culture, has been annexed by Chinatown, leaving nothing but a legend and a strip of restaurants that cater to tourists. There's no place like it left in America, you might think. Not true. The real Little Italy is alive and well in Bensonhurst, Brooklyn, centered around Eighteenth Avenue, which was recently renamed Cristoforo Colombo Boulevard. My first book was about The Neighborhood, Little Italy. This one is about Going Home, about celebrating or reestablishing The Connection—to Italy and to the places where Italy is still alive in America.

It's not just the old people who keep The Connection alive out of nostalgia for some distant, fading past. The Connection is vital, intense, present in everyday life.

On the streets of Bensonhurst, you can hear kids talking to their parents in dialect. In the churches, they have altar boys who speak in broken English—about their *fearsta commooniun*, and so forth—because their first language is Sicilian. The satellite dishes on houses and apartment buildings are not for CBS or Fox but to pick up RAI and Radio Maria, Italian television and radio beamed direct from the mother country.

There's an old tradition in Brooklyn of the "clubhouses" that's still going strong. Residents of each town stick together, forming civic organizations with their fellow immigrants—the Castellammarese have their club, the Catanese have theirs, the people from Ragusa, Vizzini, Baucina have theirs. They call themselves Figli di ("Sons of") Ragusa, Figli di Vizzini, and so forth. Some of these towns are small—nobody outside Sicily has even heard of them—but they have a big presence in Brooklyn because that's where their people are. Sometimes there may even be more people here than in the village back home!

Agnello con Finocchietto Siciliano

Sicilian Lamb with Wild Fennel

I remember that when I was growing up, my father was very strict and he had a temper. He was also a creature of habit who insisted on having certain dishes on certain days of the week. This simple lamb preparation was a Thursday dish, and we always ate it with beans. One Thursday, we had the beans but no lamb. My father got mad and slammed his hand down on the table, accidentally smacking the corner of the plate of beans, sending them flying in all directions. It took us weeks to clean the beans off the ceiling, the lights, the windows, and everything else.

About a month later, my Aunt Mary was sitting in the kitchen, gazing at a statue of the Madonna we had set up in the corner. She stared for a while, took off her glasses, cleaned the lenses, rubbed her eyes, and finally exclaimed, "Look, it's a miracle!" My grandmother said, "What are you talking about? Are you crazy?" "I'm telling you," Aunt Mary said, "it's a miracle. The Madonna grew a wart." On closer examination, it was no miracle but one of my father's beans that had stuck to her face.

The *finochietto* or "wild fennel" that grows in the mountains of Sicily is virtually impossible to get in the United States, so I've adapted the recipe to use regular domesticated fennel. The baby fennel, which is available here in America, is something a little different, but it's definitely an acceptable substitute.

2 medium fennel bulbs, trimmed and cut into medium dice

3 small spring lamb shoulders, bone in, about 2¼ pounds each

3 tablespoons extra-virgin olive oil

1 medium onion, peeled and chopped

Salt and freshly ground black pepper

2 cloves garlic, peeled and crushed

½ cup dry white wine

Blanch the fennel in 2 cups of lightly salted boiling water for 3 minutes. Drain, reserve the cooking liquid, and set the fennel aside.

Cut the lamb into 9 even pieces (3 per shoulder). Place the olive oil over medium heat in a skillet large enough to hold all the lamb and sauté the lamb pieces until lightly browned, about 8 minutes. Add the onion to the pan and cook until wilted and lightly browned, about 4 to 5 minutes. Add the garlic and cook for 2 more minutes. Season to taste with salt and pepper.

Deglaze the pan with the wine, cooking until it is evaporated, about 2 to 3 minutes. Add the fennel and 2 cups of the fennel cooking liquid, cover the pan, and allow to simmer over low heat for 1 hour, adding more liquid if it gets too dry. After 1 hour, if there is still liquid in the pan, uncover and allow it to reduce until it just glazes the lamb. (The point is to time it right, so that there is very little pourable liquid left in the pan, just a coating for the lamb.) Serve—with some of my father's beans on the side if you like (potatoes would also do).

Serves 6

Coniglio all'Agrodolce

Sweet-and-Sour Rabbit

For the average American, rabbit is not at the top of their list of favorite foods. In the past, we just didn't see it that often in meat markets; maybe occasionally on the menu at an haute cuisine establishment. Now people are coming around to the idea. The meat is light in color, mildly flavored, quite firm, lean, and it lends itself very well to this type of sweet-and-sour preparation. You can find it fresh in quality meat markets, or frozen, often at the supermarket. If not available, your butcher should be able to order it easily. (In Sicily, they raise rabbits to eat, not just as pets.)

This is a very popular preparation that is guaranteed to be finger-licking good. If you can't overcome the idea that it's rabbit, substitute chicken thighs; they're almost as good. But I would always urge you to go ahead and give rabbit a try.

With the sweet-and-sour flavors, the cinnamon and hot peppers, this dish certainly illustrates the "exotic" Middle Eastern influence on Sicilian cuisine.

1 rabbit, about 3 pounds, cut into 8 pieces
½ lemon
2 bay leaves
¼ cup pure olive oil

For the sweet-and-sour sauce
1 medium onion, peeled and sliced
1 pound Italian plum tomatoes, peeled, seeded, and diced
3 tablespoons granulated sugar
1 cup red wine vinegar
⅛ teaspoon ground cinnamon
1 cup green olives, pitted and cut into quarters
½ cup capers, rinsed

¼ cup finely ground almond flour, lightly toasted in a 250°F. oven

Place the rabbit pieces in a saucepan, add the lemon half and the bay leaves, cover with water, and bring to a boil over medium heat; lower the heat and allow to simmer for 5 minutes. Drain well. In a skillet over medium-high heat, sauté the rabbit pieces in the olive oil, turning them so they are well browned all over, about 4 to 5 minutes. Remove the rabbit with a slotted spoon and set aside.

TO PREPARE THE SAUCE: Add the onion to the same pan and cook over medium-high heat until lightly browned, about 5 minutes. Add the tomatoes, lower the heat to medium, and cook for 8 minutes. In a separate bowl, dissolve the sugar in the vinegar and stir in the cinnamon. Add the mixture to the pan along with the olives and capers.

Return the rabbit pieces to the pan, sprinkle with the almond flour, cover, and simmer over low heat for 20 minutes. Adjust the seasonings and serve.

Serves 4

Falsomagro

Stuffed Meat Roll

This is a larger version of *bracciole*, a dish that is very familiar to anyone with a southern Italian connection. Flank steak is another one of the tougher but tastier cuts of beef that, in this recipe, is pounded thin, made into a roll, and braised in wine and stock to bring out all of its delicious potential. This roll works equally well cooked in a good tomato sauce, as in the bracci-ole recipe on page 133. You can also have fun adding some of your favorite ingredients to the stuffing.

One tip: After cooking the roll, my grand-mother always removes it from the broth and al-lows it to come to room temperature, which makes slicing it much easier. On one occasion, my grandmother had three of the rolls cooling. When she went into the other room for a minute, Gino, our German shepherd, helped himself to one, string and all. My grandmother always said he was more Italian than German, anyway. So let it cool, but don't let the dog get at it.

3 large eggs

½ cup milk

¼ cup chopped fresh Italian parsley

½ cup freshly grated Parmesan cheese

Salt and freshly ground black pepper to taste

1½ pounds flank steak, butterflied and pounded thin (have your butcher do this for you)

¼ pound prosciutto, thinly sliced

½ cup pure olive oil

1 large onion, peeled and thinly sliced

3 tablespoons all-purpose flour

2 cups dry red wine

3½ cups beef broth (if using canned, use low-sodium stock)

Mix the eggs, milk, parsley, Parmesan, salt, and pepper in a bowl. Over medium heat in a non-stick skillet, cook the mixture into two pancakes. Together, they should be large enough to cover most of the flank steak.

Lay the steak out flat and place the pan-cakes on top of it, then cover them with the slices of prosciutto, leaving a small border of steak around the edges. Roll up the steak and tie the roll with butcher's twine.

Place the olive oil in a heavy-bottomed saucepan over medium-high heat. Place the roll in the pan and sear it first and then lower the heat to medium to brown it all over. Add the onion to the pan and brown it along with the meat roll. When the meat and onion are al-most done, sprinkle them with the flour, stirring well. (The flour serves to thicken the broth later, but by browning it at this stage, its starchy taste is eliminated.) When everything is well browned, deglaze the pan with the wine. Add the broth, bring to a boil, cover, and lower the heat. Allow to simmer for 60 minutes or until the meat roll is tender. Poke it with a skewer or big serving fork and if this pulls out with little resistance, the roll is done. Remove the roll from the pan, slice it, spoon the sauce from the pan over it, and serve.

Serves 8

Uccelletti di Campagna

Grilled Brochettes of Pork

I have a good friend named Joe who comes from the same town as my father, Castellammare del Golfo. Joe has introduced me to many a fine recipe, including this one. Joe is also a great storyteller. He told me one about this eighty-year-old man from Castellammare. He hadn't seen the old guy in a long time. One day he came upon him and he was crying. "What's wrong?" Joe asked. "My wife, she passed away," the old man answered. Joe immediately gave his condolences. "It's all right," the man said, "she died about nine years ago." He went on to explain how he remarried a young girl half his age, how she cared for him, how she cooked for him, and, oh, how she loved him. "Mamma mia!" Joe exclaimed, "so what's the problem?" The man cried out, "I forget where I live!"

This recipe is a very savory way to prepare pork. It, too, has a hint of the exotic, with the intriguing combination of sage, ginger, and cinnamon alongside two staples, garlic and olive oil. *Uccelletti*, by the way, means "little birds," a traditional Italian way of referring to these delicious little bundles.

6 cloves garlic, peeled and chopped

2 tablespoons chopped fresh sage

1 tablespoon freshly grated ginger

½ teaspoon ground cinnamon

1 tablespoon extra-virgin olive oil

8 slices pork, 3 ounces each, from the loin, pounded into scallops

Salt and freshly ground black pepper

8 thin slices prosciutto

Sixteen 1½-inch cubes stale bread

1 cup extra-virgin olive oil

8 thin slices pancetta, cut in half

16 bamboo skewers, soaked in water

Mix the garlic, sage, ginger, cinnamon, and olive oil together to make a paste. Set aside.

Season each scallop of pork with salt and pepper. Using the back of a teaspoon, gently spread an even amount of the garlic paste over each scallop. Lay a slice of prosciutto over each scallop and then cut the scallop in half. Roll each up, starting at the short end.

Brush each bread cube with olive oil and wrap it with half a slice of pancetta. On the bamboo skewers, alternate the pork rolls and the bread, leaving a tiny space between each. Grill on a barbecue or under your kitchen broiler for 4 minutes per side. Serve immediately.

Serves 8

Prosciutto

Prosciutto or "pro-shoot," as we say in Brook-aleena, means "ham." The crucial distinction here is between *prosciutto cotto* ("cooked") and *prosciutto crudo* ("raw"). The cooked version is boiled, pretty much exactly what you get when you order a good old American ham-and-cheese sandwich. The "raw" stuff, genuine imported prosciutto crudo, is one of our great Italian delicacies that has become more common in America as American palates have become a little more adventurous. Prosciutto crudo is the hind leg of a pig, cured instead of cooked by salting and air-drying it for thirteen months. It is served thinly sliced, either in sandwiches *(panini)* or as an appetizer with melon or figs.

Quality prosciutto strikes a perfect balance between sweetness and saltiness, between the lean, dry meat on the inside and the rich, smooth fat found in a small layer around the outside. It needs to be eaten very soon after slicing, otherwise it dries up. You can store it for a few days carefully enclosed in wax paper and then sealed in plastic wrap or a Ziploc bag, but why wait? Prosciutto often finds its way into recipes for other meats that can use a little of its flavor and its fat. When you do cook with it, be aware that it has plenty of its own salt, so go easy on any additional salt you add to the dish.

The best prosciutto crudo comes from Parma, where the pigs are fed on the whey that's left over from making Parmesan cheese. The meat is mild and delicate and its name has a nice ring to it: Prosciutto di Parma.

Another superior variety of prosciutto comes from San Daniele, a small town in the mountainous Friuli area of northeastern Italy. It is redder in color and slightly saltier than the Parma ham. Around San Daniele, the pigs are allowed to roam free and gorge themselves on acorns, giving their meat a distinctive flavor.

A third excellent type of prosciutto comes from Berico-Euganeo, a section of the Veneto (the province of Venice). It is rose-colored and even sweeter than the Parma variety.

Gaddina alla Diavola

Grilled Chicken in Pepper, Olive Oil, and Lemon

Who doesn't love barbecued chicken, especially when it's prepared as simply and deliciously as this? My family has passed this recipe down through the generations forever. Recently, my grandmother developed an innovation that can make your life much easier when marinating: Just put all the ingredients in a Ziploc bag—no fuss, no muss. If you don't have an outdoor grill or it's out of season, you can use the broiler in your oven instead.

In Italian, *alla diavola*, which is applied to many different types of dishes, translates to "devil-style," which means hot and spicy. Sicily has a hot climate, and like other hot parts of the world, you'll find a lot of spice in the cuisine. This recipe is a good example of that; of course, you can adjust the heat by using more or less pepper.

> **1 chicken, about 3½ pounds**
> **⅓ cup fresh lemon juice**
> **1 tablespoon crushed black peppercorns**
> **4 cloves garlic, peeled and crushed**
> **4 tablespoons extra-virgin olive oil**
> **2 teaspoons salt**

Cut the chicken into 8 pieces, splitting the breast and cutting off the legs and wings. Place the chicken pieces, along with the lemon juice, peppercorns, garlic, and olive oil, in a casserole or Ziploc bag, mix very well, and cover (or lock). Allow to marinate in the refrigerator for 2 hours, stirring periodically.

Remove the chicken from the marinade and season it with the salt.

Prepare a grill with the rack about 8 inches from the fire. Grill the chicken on one side until golden brown (not black), periodically brushing it with the marinade, about 12 minutes. Turn the chicken over, baste again, and cook for 15 more minutes. If you run out of marinade, you can finish basting with a little olive oil. If using the broiler, cook the chicken for the same amount of time. Remove the chicken to a platter and serve immediately.

Serves 4

Serving suggestion: Apply the same marinade to some vegetables, grill them, and serve alongside the chicken. The chicken also goes very well with a salad of seasonal mixed greens.

Polpettone

Sicilian Meat Loaf

Meat loaf? That's right, we eat meat loaf in Sicily, and there's never a complaint because our recipe is so good. What's the key to a great meat loaf? The same thing that makes for great meatballs—the bread, of course. Some people think that 100 percent meat is better, that anybody who puts bread in their meat loaf is cheating. Nothing could be further from the truth. Meat loaf must have the bread to stay moist. And stale bread is always better, so stop throwing it away, and try it in this recipe.

¾ pound ground beef

¾ pound ground pork

¾ pound ground veal

¼ cup chopped fresh mint

¼ cup chopped fresh Italian parsley

½ cup freshly grated Parmesan cheese

3 large eggs

2 cups stale bread cubes, soaked in milk to reconstitute

Salt and freshly ground black pepper to taste

2 tablespoons pure olive oil

1 medium onion, peeled and chopped

1 cup Chicken Stock (page 216)

2 sprigs fresh rosemary

2 sprigs fresh sage

Combine all the meat in a bowl with the mint, parsley, Parmesan, eggs, bread, salt, and pepper. Mix well and form into a large loaf shape, about 12 by 3 inches. Allow to sit for at least 15 minutes.

Preheat the oven to 350°F.

Place the olive oil in a baking pan over medium heat and sauté the onion until lightly browned. Stir in the stock and place the meat loaf in the pan, along with the sprigs of rosemary and sage. Bake for 40 minutes or until well browned on top. Remove from the oven and discard the rosemary and sage sprigs. Slice the meat loaf ½ inch thick, place it on a warm platter, spoon the onions over, and serve.

Serves 8

Serving suggestions: This is another hearty dish that makes for a great main course but works equally well as a leftover, warmed up or at room temperature, or as a snack, or between two pieces of bread to make a sandwich. Additional suggestion: Heat up some of your favorite (spicy) tomato sauce and ladle it on top.

Gaddina alla Creta

Chicken Baked in Clay

This is a very old recipe that dates back to Roman times. I've come across it in one form or another throughout Italy. This particular version came from Sicily, where I saw an old woman collecting river clay for it.

Now, back home you're not going to the nearest river to collect mud, but you will have to make a trip to your local arts-and-crafts store to purchase some nontoxic pottery clay. You'll also need a large piece of parchment paper to cover the chicken before you encase it in clay. There's nothing quite like the moment when you bring this dish to the table and break it open with a hammer. You will truly amaze your guests! Then when they taste it, they'll be even more amazed, since this method of cooking seals in all the juices, making it one of the most moist and flavorful roast chickens they'll ever taste.

1 chicken, about 3½ pounds

1 sprig fresh rosemary

4 fresh sage leaves

2 links sweet Italian sausage, removed from the casings

Salt and freshly ground black pepper

20 thin slices pancetta

One 3-pound box nontoxic pottery clay

Wash the chicken inside and out, then dry it well. Stuff the cavity of the bird with the rosemary, sage, and sausage meat. Season the outside with salt and pepper and lay the slices of pancetta across the breast. Carefully envelop the entire bird within a large piece of parchment paper, being sure it is securely enclosed and the paper has no holes.

Preheat the oven to 425°F.

Roll the clay out between 2 pieces of plastic wrap into a circle ¼ inch thick and large enough to cover the chicken. Remove the plastic and place the parchment-wrapped bird in the center, breast side up. Fold the clay around the chicken, completely sealing it inside. Place the chicken on a baking sheet and bake it in the oven for 1 hour and 10 minutes.

Remove the chicken in clay from the oven, bring it to the table, and crack the clay open with a mallet or the blunt end of a knife. Peel off the clay, unwrap the chicken, carve, and serve immediately with the stuffing on the side.

Serves 4

Gaddina alla Palermitana

Chicken in Bread Crumb Sauce

Now we're talking! This wonderful recipe was shown to me by my Aunt Giulia, a great cook with a legendary temper. She used the dish as a peacemaker. Allow me to explain. Whenever anyone would cross her, she had a ritual. First, she would put a picture of the pope under one arm and grab a rosary in her hand. Then, with her free hand, she would give you the horns—a gesture that, if you don't know what it means, refer to page 131—and make a noise that sounded like "Zit! Zit! Zit!" To top it off, she would give you the *malocchio* ("evil eye").

Now, you have to understand, this is serious business, giving somebody the whammy like that. Over the centuries in Sicily, wars have been fought over less. Aunt Giulia would eventually calm down and realize what she had done. To make peace with the person who got whammied she would prepare them a meal that included this, her favorite chicken recipe. Okay, I know what you're thinking: "Is this guy for real? He must be making these people up!" Oh yes, these people are for real, and they're my family, so be careful what you say about them. Otherwise, "Zit! Zit! Zit!"

1 chicken, about 3½ pounds

For the bread crumbs

18 sprigs fresh Italian parsley, leaves only, finely chopped

3 cloves garlic, peeled and finely chopped

1 cup bread crumbs, lightly toasted in a skillet

1 sprig fresh oregano, leaves only, chopped

Salt and freshly ground black pepper

For the sauce

2 cloves garlic, peeled and finely chopped

Juice of 4 lemons

1 sprig fresh oregano, leaves only, chopped

2½ cups extra-virgin olive oil

Salt and freshly ground black pepper

For the salad

1 large bunch curly endive, washed and cut into 2-inch pieces (chicory is an acceptable substitute)

1 head radicchio, washed and cut into 2-inch pieces

2 small fennel bulbs, washed and cut into small strips

12 small red radishes, washed and trimmed

18 Gaeta olives, pitted

10 tablespoons extra-virgin olive oil

5 tablespoons red wine vinegar

Salt and freshly ground black pepper

Preheat the oven to 350°F. Place a heavy-bottomed skillet in the oven for about 5 minutes to heat it up.

Wash the chicken well, inside and out, and pat dry. Using a sharp knife, cut through the chicken along each side of the backbone, then remove the backbone. Open up the chicken and flatten it out.

TO PREPARE THE BREAD CRUMBS: Place all the ingredients for the bread crumbs in a bowl and mix well. Coat the chicken with half the bread crumb mixture, pressing in as much of it as possible and reserving the other half. Set aside.

TO PREPARE THE SAUCE: Combine the garlic, lemon juice, oregano, and olive oil in a bowl and mix well. Season with salt and pepper. Remove the hot skillet from the oven and place 1 tablespoon of the sauce in it. Place the chicken in the skillet, skin side down. Cover the chicken with the remaining bread crumbs. Pour 6 tablespoons of the sauce over the chicken and place it in the oven to bake for 15 minutes. Pour 4 more tablespoons of sauce over the chicken and bake for another 10 minutes. Gently turn the chicken over and spoon the remaining sauce on top, baking for another 30 minutes.

TO PREPARE THE SALAD: While the chicken is cooking, mix the endive, radicchio, fennel, and the whole radishes in a bowl. Right before serving, add the olives and whisk together the olive oil, vinegar, salt, and pepper. Spoon the dressing over the salad and toss well.

Remove the chicken from the oven, cut it into pieces, and place it on a warm serving platter. Spoon all the bread crumbs out of the pan onto the platter and serve with the salad on the side.

Serves 4

A NOTE ABOUT BREAD CRUMBS

There is an important distinction between fresh bread crumbs and store-bought ones that is not always made in cookbooks—to the detriment of many recipes. Fresh bread crumbs are made at home by breaking up pieces of fresh bread in a food processor. The prepared bread crumbs you buy in a grocery are an entirely different ingredient.

Quagghia all' Melagrana

Roasted Quail with Pomegranate

In Sicily, there are many of what we Americans might consider exotic—or at least not typically Italian—ingredients. Pomegranates are among them and they find their way into a number of recipes. *Melagrana* means "seeded apple" in Italian. The seeds themselves are edible as is the soft, juicy red pod that surrounds them, but you have to pick apart the rest of the fruit to get to the good part. Due to its unique structure and numerous seeds, the pomegranate has had symbolic significance since ancient times.

In Greek mythology, Persephone found herself condemned to spend half the year in the underworld because she unwittingly ate a pomegranate seed. Don't worry, you can try this recipe; they stopped sending people down there sometime after the Greeks left.

Pomegranates come from the interior of Sicily and they give this dish delightful hints of sweet and tart flavors. In the United States, they are grown in California and are available from late September right through wintertime.

8 whole quail, about 2½ pounds total, legs tied together with string (see Note)

2 tablespoons unsalted butter

3 tablespoons extra-virgin olive oil

1 medium onion, peeled and chopped

1 ripe tomato, peeled, seeded, and chopped

2 cups Chicken Stock (page 216)

4 cups pomegranate seeds, from about 5 pomegranates

Salt and freshly ground black pepper to taste

4 sprigs fresh Italian parsley, leaves only, washed and chopped

In a large skillet over medium-high heat, sauté the quail in the butter and 2 tablespoons of the olive oil, browning them completely on all sides. Remove the quail from the skillet, pour off the excess fat, and keep warm on a covered platter on top of the stove.

In the same skillet over medium heat, sauté the onion in the remaining olive oil for about 15 minutes or until softened and lightly browned. Add the tomatoes and stock, return the quail to the skillet, lower the heat, and add all but ½ cup of the pomegranate seeds. Cover the pan and allow to simmer for 15 minutes or until tender. Remove the quail, pull off the strings, and keep them warm in the covered platter. Strain the sauce to remove the seeds and place it over high heat in the same pan. Reduce the sauce to 1 cup; this should take about 15 minutes. Arrange the quail on a warm serving platter. Season the sauce with salt and pepper to taste, add the parsley and remaining seeds, pour the sauce over the quail, and serve.

Serves 4

Note: Quail should be readily available fresh at your meat market or, if not, then frozen or to order. You can also try subbing small ducks.

Spezzatino di Vitello all'Olive e Funghi

Veal Stew with Olives and Mushrooms

The cheaper cuts, especially when you're talking about veal, are the more flavorful ones. They certainly take longer to cook, but let's be honest here, a milk-fed veal chop is not the most flavorful cut of veal. A shoulder of veal will fit the bill if you are on a budget or just plain don't like to spend the money. You can substitute any shoulder or other inexpensive cut or stew meat—try oxtail or venison for a little something different—to produce this typical Sicilian dish.

By the way, I learned this recipe from my great-grandmother. At every family gathering or holiday, she would make an announcement: "I want everybody to know, I won't be a-here next-a year!" As a young kid, I always wondered where she was going. She didn't seem to be the traveling type.

4 tablespoons extra-virgin olive oil

1 small onion, peeled and finely chopped

¼ pound slab bacon, diced

2 cloves garlic, peeled and thinly sliced

Pinch of crushed red pepper flakes

1 pound veal shoulder, cut into 1½-inch cubes

Salt and freshly ground black pepper

½ cup dry white wine

2 cups fresh white mushrooms, cleaned and cut into quarters

10 green olives in brine, washed, drained, pitted, and roughly chopped

Place 3 tablespoons of the olive oil in a large heavy-bottomed casserole over medium heat. Sauté the onion and bacon in it for 6 to 7 minutes or until the onion is lightly browned. Add the garlic, red pepper flakes, and the veal, raising the heat and lightly browning the veal. Season with salt and pepper, add the wine, lower the heat, cover the pot, and allow the veal to simmer for 45 minutes. If the liquid evaporates too quickly, add a little water.

While the veal is cooking, place a skillet over high heat and sauté the mushrooms in the remaining 1 tablespoon of olive oil for 3 to 4 minutes. Season with salt and pepper, remove from the pan, and set aside.

When the meat is fork tender, add the mushrooms and the olives, mix gently, and serve hot.

Serves 4

Wines of the South

Food and wine—they go together like smoke and fire, love and romance, spaghetti and meatballs. Seriously, though, there's nothing I hate more than a wine snob and nothing I respect more than a true wine lover. The people who impress me are the ones who ask for some of the lesser-known but equally delicious wines of southern Italy and Sicily. They are names we'll all become more familiar with as time goes by and as the American wine market continues to broaden its horizons. The wines of southern Italy and Sicily are less expensive—with plenty priced around ten dollars—but don't let that fool you: Quite a few of them are truly world-class. Here's a sampling:

Not so far from Castellammare in Alcamo, part of the "Golden Crescent" by the gulf, they produce very fine white wines.

Over in the Abruzzi, the mountainous province east of Rome, you find the excellent Montepulciano d'Abruzzo reds as well as the lesser-known Trebbiano d'Abruzzo whites. From Puglia, the heel of the boot, look for Aglianico del Vulture reds, not to mention the renowned Salice Salentino reds made by Cosimo Taurino and other equivalent producers.

Irpinia, the part of Campania that includes Avellino, is the home of Taurasi, known among wine connoisseurs as "the Barolo of the South," a wine that can happily age ten to twenty years. The Mastroberardino family of Atripaldi is the best-known producer; they also make two fine white wines: Greco del Tufo and Fiano.

The two biggest names in Sicily, made by families of ancient nobility that produce world-class wines, are Regaleali (the Tasca family) and Duca di Salaparuta. You've probably heard of Corvo red and white, the Duca di Salaparuta's mass-market products that are perfectly good table wines. They also make Duca Enrico, a super-premium red wine that rivals the great Bordeaux and Barolos. This is a special-occasion bottle: Save it for that Easter feast when you roast the whole baby lamb.

verdure

Vito Pesce, my great-grandfather's cousin

With its mild climate, long, hot summers, and rich volcanic soil, it's no surprise that Naples is a haven for great vegetable cuisine. Reflecting our dual themes of Naples and Sicily, you'll see plenty of vegetables I consider "typical" in the *cucina napolitana*— beans, fennel, cauliflower, tomatoes, tomatoes, and more tomatoes. Meanwhile, in Sicily you'll encounter some of the spicy, sweeter, more "exotic" flavors. Either way, you're going to use plenty of garlic and olive oil, which happen to be two of the healthiest and best-tasting foods known to man. So stock up!

In Italy, rather than spooning the vegetables onto individual plates alongside the entrées, people typically serve them on two or three communal platters to be passed around the table, usually at some point after the main course has been served. The same amount of attention and care is lavished on preparation of the vegetables as on the appetizers, pastas, and meats; they are given equal weight in the meal and treated virtually as a separate course.

When it comes to vegetables, nothing is taken for granted, and freshness is the most important criterion. Greengrocers painstakingly display bins of fresh fruits and vegetables that invite the customer in from the street. You approach the shop or stand with an eye for what looks best today and how it might fit into your meal plans. In Sicily, they have a great tradition of vendors who come around to each neighborhood with wagonloads of fresh seasonal produce. In the warmer months, all over the country, you'll see roadside stands selling fruits and vegetables. And then there are the markets. . . .

In Sicily, if you want to find just about any vegetable under the sun, you go to the Vucciria market in Palermo. It's there that you hear a chorus with two resounding themes: fresh seafood and fresh vegetables.

Many Italians tend their kitchen gardens devotedly, and this practice has most definitely crossed the Atlantic. In the backyards of my native Brooklyn you see Italians cultivating small patches of earth to grow fresh greens and herbs and tomatoes for use in their home kitchens, just like back in the old country. From the garden to the kitchen to the plate—all in a day.

Bietole all'Agro

Swiss Chard with Olive Oil and Lemon

Swiss chard is a very versatile green that turns up in a lot of Italian dishes. It comes from the beet family and is sweeter than spinach, but chard and spinach are fairly interchangeable in recipes. Look for fresh sturdy stalks and dark green leaves. As with any green, you should try it first in the simplest preparations so as to bring out its natural flavors and then use it in more complicated dishes such as soups, tarts, ravioli, and so forth. There is a variety of chard that is red, which can also be used for this recipe.

3 pounds fresh Swiss chard, the tough bottoms of the stems discarded

Salt and freshly ground black pepper to taste

1 large lemon

4 tablespoons extra-virgin olive oil

Clean the Swiss chard by removing the stems and soaking the leaves in cold water. Cut the stems into 1-inch pieces, wash well, and begin cooking them in a large pot of boiling salted water. After about 8 minutes, add the Swiss chard leaves to the pot and cook for an additional 8 minutes. Drain the Swiss chard very well and refresh under cold water. Drain it again and squeeze out any excess water. Place the Swiss chard in a serving dish and sprinkle it with salt and pepper. Squeeze the lemon on top, spoon the olive oil over it, toss, and serve.

Serves 4

BY THE SEAT OF THEIR PANTS

Normally, it wouldn't be much of a compliment to call somebody "oily ass." You sure couldn't get away with it in my old neighborhood in Brooklyn. For Leonardo and Enrico Colavita, though, it's become a term of endearment. In case you haven't heard of them, the Colavitas are in the olive-oil business. They grew up in the village of Sant'Elia a Pianisi in the province of Campobasso, where olive millers were often called *culli unti* ("oily asses") due to their habit of wiping their hands on the seats of their pants. The stains quickly became permanent badges of their profession and the name stuck, too.

Leonardo and Enrico's father, Giovanni, and uncle, Zio Felice, were *culli unti;* when the boys took over the business, they became *culli unti,* too. They still operate the small press in their hometown, but they also travel far and wide all over southern Italy to sample and purchase the best olive oils for both domestic consumption and export. Nowadays, the Colavitas are more likely to be seen in business suits than in stained overalls, but they never forget their origins and the stringent standards represented by the men with oily hands and pants.

Patate alla Contadina

Country-Style Potatoes

This recipe is like a warm potato salad. My people back on the farms and in the villages have been making it for years and this is how it was passed down to me. Tossing the potatoes while still hot helps ensure a total melding of all the flavors. I always recommend cooking them with the skins on—for added flavor and to prevent excess water seepage. To peel them hot, just keep those fingers moving fast and you shouldn't get burned. One final piece of advice: Use boiling potatoes, such as Red Bliss or new potatoes, not the Idaho baking potatoes or russets, which become mealy and dry and fall apart when you boil them.

1 pound medium boiling potatoes

Coarse-grained sea salt or kosher salt

1 large clove garlic, peeled and chopped

10 sprigs fresh Italian parsley, leaves only, chopped

¼ cup extra-virgin olive oil

Salt and freshly ground black pepper

Cook the potatoes in a large pot of boiling salted water until tender, about 35 minutes.

Mix the garlic, parsley, and olive oil together in a bowl. Season with salt and pepper to taste.

Once the potatoes are cooked, drain them, peel the skins off while still hot, and cut them into 1-inch cubes. While still hot, add them to the bowl with the other ingredients and toss. Serve warm or cold.

Serves 3

Pomodori al Forno

Baked Tomatoes with Garden Herbs

You know how I feel about bread crumbs: I love their texture and I love how they accentuate the flavors of fresh herbs, garlic, and olive oil. This dish works very well with tomatoes that are firm and maybe not so ripe, because they hold the stuffing well and don't fall apart so easily in the oven.

6 large plum tomatoes

Coarse-grained sea salt

35 sprigs fresh Italian parsley

30 fresh basil leaves

10 fresh mint leaves

2 cloves garlic, peeled

4 tablespoons extra-virgin olive oil, plus additional (about 6 tablespoons) for drizzling

Salt and freshly ground black pepper

4 tablespoons fresh bread crumbs

Cut the tomatoes in half crosswise, remove all the seeds, and sprinkle a little coarse salt into each cavity. Place the tomatoes upside down in a colander and allow to drain for 20 minutes.

Preheat the oven to 375°F.

Lightly oil the bottom of a baking dish. Chop the parsley, basil, mint, and garlic together, place in a bowl, and mix with the 4 tablespoons of olive oil. Season with salt and pepper.

Lightly rinse the tomatoes and dry them out. Fill the tomatoes with the herbs, top with bread crumbs, and drizzle the remaining olive oil over all. Place in the baking dish and bake for 1 hour, until golden brown. Serve hot or at room temperature.

Serves 6

Fagioli al Fiasco

Cannellini in a Flask

This recipe employs a very old technique that is more than just a gimmick. In classic French cuisine, it's called a bain-marie, where you place a cooking vessel inside a pot or pan of hot water to provide gentle heat all around. The key to the method in this case is that it uses very little liquid so the beans retain all of their flavor. I call for a wide-mouthed wine flask, but if you can't find it, you can substitute a large mason jar, which is what we did for the photograph, or even a ceramic crock. One precaution: When you start, make sure the liquids on the outside of the flask and on the inside are both cold so that you don't crack the flask.

This is a really fun recipe and the best part, as with chicken in clay or fish in a bag, is checking out the reaction from your guests when you bring the whole flask to the table.

1 pound dried cannellini (Great Northern) beans

1 tablespoon all-purpose flour

3 ounces pancetta, diced

¼ cup extra-virgin olive oil

2 cloves garlic, peeled

4 fresh Italian plum tomatoes, peeled, cut in half lengthwise, and seeded

10 fresh basil leaves

Salt and freshly ground black pepper

Soak the beans overnight in cold water with the flour. (Place the flour in the pot first, then whisk as you pour in the water to avoid any possible lumps.) Drain the beans well and rinse.

Place the beans in the flask with enough cold water to cover by 1 inch. Add the pancetta, olive oil, whole garlic, tomatoes, and basil. Season with salt and pepper, stir well, and place the flask in a large stockpot with cold water. Cover the entire assembly loosely with aluminum foil and place the pot over medium heat and allow to simmer for 3½ hours. Do not add liquid to the flask during the cooking. If you need to add water to the stockpot, add boiling water, not cold water.

When the beans are done, remove the flask from the pot, bring it to the table, and serve.

Serves 6

Note: The beans must be soaked overnight in advance. They really benefit from the long, slow simmering in the water bath. And you can successfully reheat them the next day or serve them at room temperature in a salad.

Gatto di Patate

Neapolitan Potato Cake

This dish reminds me of when my Uncle Anthony, who was a priest in the Vatican, came from Italy. Considering his proximity to the pope, his arrival was very important in our family. A feast was planned to celebrate his arrival, and this dish, one of his favorites, was featured. There was one problem. His niece, my cousin Carmela, who had been married for two years, had gotten a divorce and nobody had told him. When he asked where her husband, Joey, was a great hush fell over the table. Everybody looked around the room, afraid to tell him the truth. His brother Frank couldn't bear to lie to him. "Anthony," he said, "I'm afraid they have parted." "Parted? You meana divorce?" People's mouths were wide open; they all shook their heads yes. "Gooda," His Holiness Father Anthony responded. "I never liked-a that guy anyway!"

2 pounds baking potatoes, peeled and quartered

8 tablespoons (¼ pound) unsalted butter, cut into small pieces

5 ounces freshly grated Parmesan cheese

¼ pound prosciutto, finely diced

2 large eggs, beaten

Salt and freshly ground black pepper

¼ cup chopped fresh Italian parsley

½ pound mozzarella cheese, cut into medium dice

3 tablespoons extra-virgin olive oil

1 cup bread crumbs

Cook the potatoes in boiling salted water until fork tender, about 20 minutes. Drain the potatoes and put them through a ricer. Mix 5 tablespoons of the butter, along with the Parmesan, prosciutto, eggs, salt, pepper, and parsley, into the potatoes.

Preheat the oven to 375°F.

Place the mozzarella in a bowl, pour in the olive oil, season with salt and pepper, then mix well.

Grease the bottom of a 9-inch round baking dish with 1 tablespoon of the butter. Line the buttered dish with bread crumbs to cover; spread half the potato mixture around the sides and over the bottom of the dish. Place the seasoned mozzarella cubes together in the middle and cover with the remaining potato mixture. Sprinkle with more bread crumbs, dot the top with the remaining butter, and bake in the oven 45 minutes or until golden brown on top. Allow to sit for 5 minutes, place a dish over the top, turn it over, and unmold the potato cake from the baking dish. Serve hot.

Serves 8

Finocchi in Sugo Finto

Fennel in Country Tomato Sauce

In the realm of vegetables, fennel and tomato form one of the most beautiful natural combinations to be found. Fresh tomatoes and fennel, sliced thin, with olive oil and vinegar dressing, make a great summer salad. Speaking of salads, try one with shaved fennel and Parmesan, a little oil and lemon juice (olive oil works, but if you really want to get fancy, try a touch of truffle oil). Fennel is also great braised, grilled, or sautéed. If you've never had cooked fennel, this recipe is a good place to start.

4 medium fennel bulbs, tops trimmed off

1 cup all-purpose flour

5 tablespoons extra-virgin olive oil

2 cloves garlic, peeled and left whole

Salt and freshly ground black pepper

2 pounds very ripe fresh plum tomatoes, passed through a food mill

Cut through the fennel bulbs vertically to create ½-inch-thick slices. Lightly flour the fennel slices, patting off the excess.

Place the olive oil over medium-high heat in a large skillet. Sauté the fennel slices about 2 minutes on each side or until they are golden brown. Sprinkle them with salt and pepper. Add the garlic and tomatoes to the pan, lower the heat, and allow them to simmer for 15 minutes, making sure that the fennel doesn't stick to the bottom of the pan. Remove from the pan and serve hot.

Serves 4

HOW TO ROAST PEPPERS

Although you can buy very good roasted peppers in jars at the supermarket or Italian deli, it's easy and fun to roast them at home. First, buy the best red, green, or yellow bell peppers from your greengrocer. Then place the pepper directly on a heat source. Roast until the skin is blackened, using the stem as a handle to turn it. Rinse the pepper under cool running water and the blackened outer skin will peel off easily. You can roast the peppers by putting them directly on the flame of one of your stovetop burners or you can put them right on top of the hot coals in your outdoor barbecue. If you're going to do it inside, make sure your kitchen is adequately ventilated, because the peppers give off a pungent aroma. Believe me, if you don't have the fan on or the windows open, everybody's going to come running and yelling "What's burning in the kitchen?!" Once the peppers are rinsed, remove the seeds and membranes from the inside and they're ready to use in a recipe. You can also serve them as part of a salad or as a side dish or condiment in their own right.

Insalata di Rinforzo Napolitana

Neapolitan Cauliflower Salad

Although it's often ignored, cauliflower is actually a very versatile, delicious, nutritious, and economical vegetable. This particular salad is traditionally served at Christmas, a very special holiday in Italy as it is all over the world. What I like about Christmas in Italy is that it lasts twelve days, climaxing on January 6, the feast of the Epiphany, when it is not Santa Claus who brings gifts to the children but La Befana—a good witch.

In Naples, they serve this salad throughout the holidays. They boil the cauliflower, carrots, and peppers, mix them up with white vinegar, hot pepper flakes, oil, anchovies, and Gaeta olives and let it pickle. It's a bracing, spicy, pick-me-up, hence the name *rinforzo* ("reinforcement"), from the verb *rinforzare* ("to strengthen"). You can find a version of it in jars at Italian delis and supermarkets under the name *insalata giardiniera* ("garden salad"). But forget about that—you should make this version at home.

This salad should be prepared well in advance of serving—I recommend 3 hours—so the vegetables and dressing have a chance to marinate and create a delicious melding of flavors.

1 head cauliflower, cut into small florets (discard the stem portions)

⅓ cup extra-virgin olive oil

3 tablespoons red wine vinegar

Salt and freshly ground black pepper

2 large sprigs fresh oregano

8 anchovy fillets, rinsed and julienned

½ cup Gaeta olives, pitted and cut in half

¼ cup capers, rinsed

1½ cups roasted red bell peppers (see page 171), seasoned with vinegar and oil

Cook the cauliflower in boiling salted water till tender, about 3 to 5 minutes. (It can also be steamed if you prefer.) Refresh under cold water and drain very well. Place the cauliflower in a bowl with the olive oil and vinegar. Season to taste with the salt and pepper. Strip the oregano leaves from the sprigs and add them to the bowl along with the anchovies, olives, and capers. Cut the peppers into narrow strips, add them to the bowl, toss well, and allow to sit for at least 3 hours at room temperature before serving.

Serves 8

Teglia d'Indivia Brasata

Braised Curly Endive with Garden Tomato

Most people have a hard time getting used to cooking greens that are usually associated with salads. Curly endive—not to be confused with chicory, which is definitely a type of lettuce—is a slightly bitter vegetable that is often overlooked and lends itself particularly well to cooking.

2 heads curly endive, washed well and dried
Salt
2 tablespoons extra-virgin olive oil
1 medium onion, peeled and finely chopped
3 ounces pancetta, finely diced
1 cup Chicken Broth (page 216)
3 plum tomatoes, peeled, seeded, and diced
Freshly ground black pepper

Blanch the heads of endive in a large pot of lightly salted boiling water for 3 minutes. Drain and squeeze the heads, then cut them into quarters lengthwise.

Place the olive oil in a large skillet over medium heat. Add the onion and pancetta and cook for 4 to 5 minutes, until the onion is soft. Add the endive quarters and sauté for 3 to 4 minutes or until they're lightly browned. Add the broth and the tomatoes, season with salt and pepper, cover, lower the heat, and simmer for 20 minutes. Remove the cover and cook for 10 more minutes, allowing the liquid to evaporate until the pan is almost completely dry. Serve hot.

Serves 4

RIPE TOMATOES

First of all, the color of ripe tomatoes should be a deep, rich red. The tomato should be fragrant around the stem, heavy for its size, soft but with no mushy spots. Tomatoes will ripen a bit after they're picked but the ones that are picked far short of ripe will probably never get there. The ones with part of the stem left on will ripen better. In Italy, toward the end of the season, in late summer or early fall, they just hack down the plant and bring it to market with all its remaining tomatoes on the vines. They always sell the little cherry tomatoes, which have an intense flavor, on the vine and sometimes they even sell them dried that way.

Brocculeddu alla Siciliana

Casserole of Broccoli and Cheese

Broccoli and cheese is just a fantastic combination. Everybody knows that broccoli is one of the healthiest vegetables around. Yet, how many kids have turned their noses up at broccoli? But melt some cheese on top and it's a different story. . . .

⅓ cup extra-virgin olive oil

1 large onion, peeled and sliced ¼ inch thick

1½ pounds broccoli, cut into florets, the tough stems peeled

Salt and freshly ground black pepper

½ cup dry red wine

12 Gaeta olives, pitted and coarsely chopped

3 anchovy fillets, coarsely chopped

1⅓ cups shredded mild provolone cheese (you can substitute caciocavallo)

Place 2 tablespoons of the olive oil in a skillet over medium heat and sauté the onion until golden. Place 2 more tablespoons of the olive oil in a separate skillet over medium heat and sauté the broccoli florets for 5 to 6 minutes. Season the broccoli with salt and pepper, add the red wine, raise the heat, and cook until the wine is reduced and the pan is almost dry.

Preheat the oven to 375°F. Lightly grease the bottom of a baking dish with olive oil and spread the onion on the bottom. Spread the broccoli over the onion, then distribute the olives, anchovies, and provolone evenly. Drizzle a small amount of olive oil over all. Bake just until the provolone is melted and bubbling, about 12 minutes. Serve hot.

Serves 6

Cannellini al Diavolo

Spicy White Beans with Tomatoes

Although most people associate Italian cuisine with such ingredients as pasta, garlic, olive oil, and tomatoes, beans are also extremely popular. My guess is that if you asked a representative sampling of one hundred Italians whether they had beans in their cupboard at a given moment, ninety-nine would say yes. And the one who said no would probably be lying! Here is a typically Sicilian way to prepare cannellini in that it adds a little bit of that fire I was talking about earlier.

In case you're looking for them in the supermarket and can't seem to find them, you should know that throughout most of America cannellini are known as Great Northern beans.

¼ cup extra-virgin olive oil

1 medium onion, peeled and chopped

5 cloves garlic, peeled and chopped

¼ pound prosciutto, finely diced

1 teaspoon crushed red pepper flakes

1 pound Swiss chard, stems finely diced, leaves cut into quarters

Salt to taste

2 cups cooked cannellini beans (canned beans are an acceptable substitute; you can also substitute any other type of bean you like, soaked overnight in advance and simmered until tender)

4 ripe plum tomatoes, peeled, seeded, and diced

¼ cup chopped fresh Italian parsley

Place the olive oil in a saucepan over medium heat and sauté the onion, garlic, and prosciutto for 4 minutes or until translucent. Add the red pepper flakes and the Swiss chard stems and cook for 2 more minutes. Add the Swiss chard leaves, season with salt, then add the beans, tomatoes, and parsley. Lower the heat, cover the pan, and cook for 7 minutes. Check the seasoning and serve hot.

Serves 8

Cacuocciuli Chini

Stuffed Artichokes with Ricotta

When I was brought up, I was taught the traditional method of stuffing artichokes, which is to pull the leaves apart, separating them enough to be able to push a bread crumb–based stuffing into the gaps. In this recipe, though, you cut the artichokes in half, braise them, and then place the ricotta-based stuffing inside. The mild flavor and smooth texture of the ricotta is balanced against the salty little chunks of salami and the grated pecorino. I did this recipe on the TV Food Network and it was a real favorite with my viewers. We got one of our biggest responses, having received about two hundred letters. By the way, you can create variations on the stuffing by substituting such items as caciocavallo for the pecorino and sorpressata or boiled ham for the salami.

3 tender medium artichokes

1 medium lemon

½ pound ricotta cheese, drained in a coffee filter for 30 minutes

1 large egg, lightly beaten

½ cup freshly grated pecorino romano cheese

8 thin slices salami, finely chopped

10 whole black peppercorns

1 teaspoon salt

2 teaspoons plus 4 tablespoons extra-virgin olive oil

½ cup fresh bread crumbs

Pull off the tough outer leaves of the artichokes. Trim the pointy ends off the leaves with scissors, cut the artichokes in half lengthwise, and scoop out the fuzzy chokes. Cut the lemon in half and rub the artichokes with one of the halves, then place them in a bowl of cold water.

Combine the ricotta, egg, pecorino, and salami in a bowl, mixing well. Place the artichoke halves in a pot with enough water to cover. Add the juice of the other half of the lemon, the peppercorns, salt, and the 2 teaspoons of olive oil. Bring the pot to a boil over high heat, lower the heat, and allow the artichokes to simmer for 20 minutes or until tender. Remove the cooked chokes from the pot with a slotted spoon and drain them in a colander, then place on a plate to cool. When the chokes are cool, lay them on their sides and stuff the cavities with a mound of the ricotta mixture.

Preheat the oven to 375°F.

Lightly oil the bottom of an ovenproof dish, place the artichokes in it, and sprinkle each with the bread crumbs. Drizzle the artichokes with the remaining olive oil and bake in the oven until the bread crumbs are golden, about 8 to 10 minutes. Serve hot or at room temperature. They're great either way.

Serves 6

Cucuzzeddi al Cartoccio

Zucchini Baked in a Bag

This is an ancient method of cooking—not only vegetables but also meat and fish (see page 100). The funny part is trying to find a paper bag that doesn't have the name of the supermarket on it. Try explaining that to the checkout person while you're going through their supply of bags. It's OK, just tell them Dave Ruggerio sent you!

¼ cup extra-virgin olive oil

6 small zucchini, washed and ends cut off

Salt and freshly ground black pepper

4 cloves garlic

For the sauce

3 tablespoons capers, rinsed

3 cloves garlic, peeled and finely chopped

12 sprigs fresh Italian parsley, leaves only, finely chopped

15 fresh mint leaves, very coarsely chopped

Salt and freshly ground black pepper

½ cup extra-virgin olive oil

Preheat the oven to 400°F.

Brush the brown paper bag, inside and outside, with olive oil. Brush the zucchini with olive oil and season with salt and pepper. Place the zucchini in the bag with the garlic and close the bag tightly. Bake the bag in the oven for 30 minutes.

TO PREPARE THE SAUCE: While the zucchini is baking, place the sauce ingredients in a bowl, mix well, and season to taste with salt and pepper.

When the zucchini are cooked, remove them from the bag, cut them into 2-inch pieces, pour the sauce over them, and allow them to marinate at room temperature for at least 1 hour, preferably 2 to 3 hours. Serve them at room temperature or reheated.

Serves 6

Funci Fritti cu Limuni e Agghiu

Fried Mushrooms with Lemon and Garlic

My love for mushrooms goes back as far as I can remember, to the family tradition of hunting wild ones. To this day, we go out into the woods in the fall in search of a few familiar varieties.

Now, it becomes a little delicate when you try to explain a potentially dangerous activity like this to the home cook. I don't think my insurance covers it, so I won't go into any details. Suffice it to say that folklore dictates throwing an old silver quarter—real silver—into the pan as you cook the mushrooms. If the coin turns dark, they're no good, you throw them out. I have no idea whether there's any scientific basis for this. I do know we've been doing it for hundreds of years, and it's worked so far. . . .

One final piece of advice: Don't drop this book and run out into the woods looking for mushrooms to try this out. Go to the store and buy yours—it's a much better guarantee.

¼ cup extra-virgin olive oil

5 cloves garlic, peeled and crushed

1 pound small button mushrooms, cleaned
    and cut in half vertically (of course,
    you can also substitute wild
    mushrooms of your choice)

Salt and freshly ground black pepper

2 medium lemons

¼ cup fresh bread crumbs

Place the olive oil in a skillet over medium heat. Add the garlic and mushrooms and cook for 8 to 10 minutes or until the mushrooms are golden brown. Season with salt and pepper to taste. Squeeze the lemons over the mushrooms. (You can wrap a lemon in a towel or a piece of cheesecloth to squeeze it, or simply squeeze through a strainer.) Sprinkle the mushrooms with the bread crumbs and stir to moisten the bread crumbs. Remove from the pan and serve immediately.

Serves 4

Carot' in Dolce-Forte

Sweet-and-Sour Carrots

Carrots are another tasty, healthy, and economical vegetable that are often either overlooked or not considered particularly Italian. Here is a full-flavored recipe that can certainly hold its own with roasted meats or grilled fish and is sweet-and-sour, Sicilian style.

1½ pounds medium carrots, peeled

8 tablespoons unsalted butter

1 tablespoon all-purpose flour

1 tablespoon granulated sugar

3 tablespoons red wine vinegar

¾ cup water

Salt and freshly ground black pepper
    to taste

Cut each carrot into 4 equal pieces, then quarter lengthwise.

Place the butter in a skillet over medium heat. When it begins to sizzle, add the flour and stir with a wooden spoon, then add the sugar, mix well, and add the vinegar, water, and carrots. Stir well and allow to simmer for 15 minutes, until the liquid evaporates, coating the carrots and they become tender. Adjust the seasoning and serve.

Serves 6

Palermo and the Vucciria Market

I love going back to the old country, and one of the reasons is that I find the atmosphere in a city like Palermo magical. It's typical of Italy in many ways; in others, it's totally different. There are palm trees all over. It's a bustling city, with crazy traffic, fast little cars and scooters everywhere. You even see the occasional horse-drawn carriage or harness dray. The residential neighborhoods of the old city are a maze of tiny streets snaking off the main thoroughfares, lined with old, whitewashed, tile-roofed apartment houses. Everywhere you look, you see juxtapositions of the ancient and the modern.

Sicily has a tradition of decorated wooden horse carts; on a recent trip, I saw a motorized tricycle-truck adorned in the same style, with multicolored bunting, sequins, and other fancy accoutrements. In the jumbled center of the city, you see the typical wrought-iron balconies jutting out over narrow alleys. Everybody hangs the laundry out to dry. (Why not save on the electric bills?)

Like other Italian cities, Palermo tends to operate at a frenetic pace, but there is always a time and place to enjoy life's simple pleasures. For me, coming from New York, it's a real treat to wind down over a cup of espresso or, on a hot day, a *granita di caffè* (basically a frozen espresso). That's what I love about the Italians. They've got energy to burn, but they also know how to slow down and take a little extra time to savor the food, the drink, the art, and the music.

Right smack in the middle of old Palermo, fanning out from the Piazza Caraciolo, is the Vucciria, one of the greatest food markets you'll ever see. Walk down those few steps off the Via Roma and you enter another world, a food lover's paradise. I can feel the excitement just writing about it.

In the Vucciria, which claims to be the oldest continuous market in Europe, they sell everything from swordfish to snails, giant zucchini to corn on the cob. The fruit and vegetable stands are enormous and laden with fresh produce from all over the island. You've got a little bit of every-thing, with a touch of the exotic: All the usual vegetables—tomatoes, peppers, lettuce, spinach and other greens, broccoli, squash, and so forth—arrayed alongside light green four-foot-long giant zucchini, something you won't ever see at your local farmers market. One wouldn't be surprised to see corn on the cob on Long Island in August, but in Palermo in June? It's there, though.

A dry goods stand in the Vucciria will sell all kinds of typical Sicilian ingredients including *mandorle* ("almonds"), *lenti* ("lentils"), *carruba* ("carob"), *mais tostado* ("toasted corn"), *fave pepate* ("spicy fava beans"), *noce di Sorrento* ("walnuts from Sorrento"), *caperi di Pantelleria* ("big salted capers from the island of Pantelle-ria"; they also grow *lenti di Pantelleria* there), *origano* (you guessed it, "oregano"), *piselli* ("split peas"), *sultanine* ("golden raisins"), and *fagioli di Spagna* ("white beans," like cannel-lini). They might also offer *fiori di fichidindia*—Sicilian for "dried fig flowers"—which can be made into a tea that's said to be beneficial to your kidneys and circulation.

The fish vendors feature impressive dis-plays of tuna and swordfish, including the heads and swords standing on end, along with other standards such as bass, cod, sardines, anchovies, and so forth. Some of them sell more exotic items such as *babbaluci* ("small sea snails"), minia-ture *scungilli* ("whelk"), and maybe even the *neonati* ("newborn fish").

You'll see plenty of people eating on the streets at the market and in other parts of Palermo. Street food—known as "take out" where I come from—is a huge part of Sicilian culture. In the big cities like Palermo and Cata-nia, in the hundreds of little seaside towns, espe-cially during holidays and street festivals, you'll see carts and stands selling seafood—octopus, mussels, oysters, clams, sea urchin, sea snails—and many other delicious snack treats.

Insalata i Cippuddi

Roasted Onion Salad, Sicilian Style

Ask the average cook what his or her favorite vegetable is and onion will rarely be the answer. It's ironic because onion is probably the most commonly used vegetable and definitely one of the most overlooked. If you have never tried cooking an onion and allowing it to stand alone, this is a great recipe to start with. Once you've tasted this, you'll be convinced. One word of caution, though: You will have onion breath!

How do you cut onions without starting to cry? You'll often hear that it's important to wet your knife but the real key is to use a *very sharp* knife. Duller knives will crush the onion, squeezing the juice out, and it's those little particles in the air that irritate your eyes, causing them to tear. The sharp knife cuts through clean, with little or no juicing.

5 medium white onions, unpeeled

6 tablespoons extra-virgin olive oil

1 clove garlic, peeled and finely chopped

¼ teaspoon crushed red pepper flakes

1 tablespoon chopped fresh Italian parsley

½ teaspoon red wine vinegar

Salt and freshly ground black pepper

Preheat the oven to 300°F.

Trim off one end of each onion and cut the onions into ½-inch slices, leaving the skin on. Lightly oil the bottom of a baking sheet, brush the onion slices with olive oil and place them on the sheet. Bake for 1 hour, then carefully turn the slices with a spatula and continue to bake for 30 more minutes. The onions should be caramelized but not burned. Using a spatula, carefully place the cooked slices onto a serving dish, removing the outside skin and any other dried-out rings. Make a vinaigrette by mixing the remaining olive oil with the garlic, red pepper flakes, parsley, 1 tablespoon of water, vinegar, and salt and pepper to taste. Spoon the vinaigrette over the onions and serve at room temperature.

Serves 6

Mulinciani a' Siciliana

Eggplant, Sicilian Style

This is a baked dish with a lot of flavor, featuring eggplant, tomatoes, and melted cheese, a quick route to a delicious eggplant casserole. It's a dish that can be reheated as a leftover, made into a sandwich between two pieces of crusty Italian bread, even used as a pasta sauce.

About ¼ cup extra-virgin olive oil

3 pounds eggplant, peeled and cut lengthwise into ¼-inch slices

Salt and freshly ground black pepper

One 32-ounce can whole peeled plum tomatoes, with their juice, crushed

1 sprig fresh oregano, leaves only, chopped

1 large bunch fresh basil

3 cups freshly grated pecorino romano cheese (Parmesan or ricotta salata cheese can be substituted)

½ teaspoon granulated sugar

continued

Place olive oil in a skillet over medium heat. (There should be enough olive oil to just coat the bottom of the pan before cooking each batch; eggplant absorbs a lot of oil, so be careful not to oversaturate it.) Sauté the slices of eggplant in small batches on both sides until golden. Season the eggplant with salt and pepper, transfer to a colander, and allow to drain.

Drain off any remaining oil from the skillet and wipe it dry. Place 3 tablespoons of olive oil in the skillet over medium heat. Add the tomatoes, oregano, 6 whole basil leaves, 2 tablespoons of the grated cheese, ½ teaspoon of sugar, salt, and pepper. Bring to a simmer and allow to cook, uncovered, for about 10 minutes.

Preheat the oven to 375°F.

Place a layer of the eggplant in a baking dish, sprinkle some grated cheese over it, followed by a few basil leaves torn in half and a little sauce. Repeat this layering procedure until all the ingredients are used. Bake for 15 minutes. Remove and serve hot.

Serves 6

Insalata Verde cogli Agrumi

Assorted Greens Salad with Citrus

What could be better—and more typically Sicilian—in the summer than a wonderful assortment of greens laced with fresh citrus? The prewashed mesclun mixes that you find in gourmet specialty stores and, increasingly, in the salad sections of your supermarkets have become very popular. They do make life a little easier, but I much prefer to create my own mix, using Boston lettuce, some red leaf, even some arugula. A lot of times, in my humble opinion, the other mesclun ends up looking like weeds somebody picked next to a highway.

In this recipe, I call for a blood orange to make it authentically Sicilian, but if you can't find one, just substitute any good eating orange.

6 cups mixed greens (see Headnote)
½ grapefruit, preferably pink
1 blood orange
¼ cup extra-virgin olive oil
3 tablespoons red wine vinegar
Salt and freshly ground black pepper
1 shallot, peeled and finely chopped

Make sure the greens are thoroughly clean. Rinse them in plenty of cold running water and dry them in a salad spinner or by placing them in a towel and spinning it around with your arm. (This latter method is a lot of fun and you can even delegate the job to a responsible kid or semiresponsible adult.)

Using a knife, peel the rinds off the grapefruit and orange, cut the fruits into segments, and place in a bowl. Squeeze into the bowl any extra juice in the remaining membranes of the fruit. Add the olive oil, vinegar, salt, pepper, and shallot. Mix well, toss with the greens, and serve immediately. (Always place the dressing on the greens just before you are ready to serve the salad; if you don't, the salad gets soggy.)

Serves 4

dolci

Nonna *presiding at the table*

As I may have told you, I'm a sucker for desserts. It's that little kid inside of me who can't ever seem to get over his sweet tooth. Nothing makes me happier than a few crunchy cookies, some *brutti ma buoni,* maybe a couple of *taralli,* alongside a cup of espresso or a well-made cassata with a nice scoop of ice cream on the side. I could skip the rest of the meal, and I know there are a lot of you out there who feel the same way.

In southern Italy and particularly Sicily, you'll find that the desserts often center on religious holidays—whether they're made at home or sold in the pastry shops or from stands at the street fairs. In this chapter, I'm providing several examples, including the Sfince di San Giuseppe and the Easter Rolls. Throughout Italy, desserts are generally simple, direct, not overly complicated. Although Italians love their cakes and pastries—which you'll see proudly laid out in the display windows and cases at the *pasticcerie* ("pastry shops")—a simple meal at home is just as likely to end with a bowl of fresh fruit or maybe a fruit salad, which they call *macedonia.* In the south, many of the desserts are fried and they call for plenty of ricotta cheese, which provides a lovely smooth texture and a pure milky richness to the fillings for cakes, pies, cassatas, and cannoli.

Granduncle Pasquale Pesce marrying Giovanna Salerni in Sant'Angelo dei Lombardi

Crostata di Ricotta

Italian Cheesecake

I have my Aunt Josephine to thank for this fabulous cheesecake recipe. She's married to my Uncle Joe (who is my grandfather Leonard Lazzarino's brother), so we just call them "Aunt and Uncle Joe." They love to go on cruises—to Italy, to the Caribbean, out into the ocean and back again. My uncle also loves to play practical jokes on my aunt. On their last cruise, there was a light switch by the headboard on my uncle's side of the bed that controlled the light in the hallway of their cabin. As they both lay in bed, she asked him to get up and turn off the light. "Not necessary," he said. "They have a 'clapper,' so all you have to do is clap your hands and the light goes off." As my aunt clapped her hands, my uncle secretly reached back and turned off the light. Aunt Josephine fell asleep and started to snore. After a while my uncle turned on the light and woke her up. "Josephine!" he said, "you're snoring is so damn loud it turned on the light." This happened two more times, until finally my aunt called down to maintenance and demanded that they disconnect the "clapper" so they could go to sleep. "You should have seen the expression on her face when she found out there was no clapper," Uncle Joe said. Needless to say, he didn't get much sleep for the rest of the night.

Which reminds me of another story. When I was growing up, we'd always give big going-away parties on board the ships for friends or family who were heading back to Italy. These affairs would last all day until the ship was ready to sail and they kicked all the nonpassengers off. Everybody would bring food and gifts and we'd have the party in the cabin on board. Well, a few years ago, I was invited to be guest chef on a cruise aboard the *QE2*, the last of the great British transatlantic liners. Everybody showed up for the party, loaded down with food, only to be informed that no visitors were allowed inside the pier. *Madonn'!* We had the party on the West Side Highway.

For the dough

1½ cups all-purpose flour

⅓ cup granulated sugar

1 extra-large egg, plus 1 egg yolk

6 tablespoons unsalted butter, cut into small cubes

For the filling

2 ounces diced mixed candied fruit peel (see Note)

2 ounces golden raisins

½ cup light rum

3 ounces blanched whole almonds

3 extra-large eggs

15 ounces ricotta cheese

Grated zest of 1 lemon

Grated zest of 1 orange

7 tablespoons granulated sugar

3 tablespoons all-purpose flour

TO PREPARE THE DOUGH: Combine the flour and sugar in a mixing bowl and make a well in the center. Put the egg, egg yolk, and butter in the well. Using a wooden spoon, mix all the ingredients together until incorporated. Do not overmix. Cover and refrigerate for at least 30 minutes.

TO PREPARE THE FILLING: Soak the fruit peel and raisins in the rum for 15 minutes. Grind the almonds in a food processor or coffee grinder until very fine. Separate one of the eggs and combine the white with the almonds, mixing very well.

Preheat the oven to 375°F.

Place the ricotta in a piece of cheesecloth or in a coffee filter inside a colander for 15 minutes to drain away any excess water. Thoroughly combine the drained ricotta with the 2 remaining eggs and egg yolk and the lemon and orange zests. Drain the candied fruit and raisins and add them to the ricotta mixture, then combine the almond mixture and the sugar, mixing well. When everything is incorporated, stir in the flour.

Butter a 9-inch springform pan. Roll out your chilled dough to a thickness of ³⁄₈ inch. Lay the dough in the buttered pan, pressing it into the corners. Allow the excess to overhang. Distribute the filling evenly inside the dough. Trim the excess dough from the perimeter of the pan, roll it out, and cut into ½-inch-wide strips. Lay the strips over the top of the filling in a crisscross pattern (optional). Bake the cake for 35 minutes, allowing it to cool for at least 30 minutes before removing from the pan. Serve cold or at room temperature.

Serves 6

Note: The recipe for candied fruit peels is in my first book, *Little Italy Cookbook.* I won't repeat it, so go out and buy the book if you want it. Otherwise, you'll have to buy some candied fruit peel.

Busie d'la Nonna

Grandma's Lies

What—my grandmother lie? She would never do that! The closest she'll ever get to fibbing is making these little sweets. In Neapolitan households, these small sweet ribbons of pastry are favorites, with many a grandmother using them to reward the children for their good behavior.

2¼ cups all-purpose flour
4 tablespoons unsalted butter, softened
1 large egg
2 tablespoons granulated sugar
Pinch of salt
5 tablespoons sweet vermouth
Vegetable oil for frying
Confectioners' sugar for dusting

Place the flour in a bowl and cut the butter into it. Add the egg, sugar, salt, and vermouth, using a wooden spoon or an electric mixer; blend until you have a smooth, fairly stiff dough. Cover the bowl with plastic wrap and place it in the refrigerator for 2 hours.

On a lightly floured surface, roll the dough out to a thickness of ⅛ inch. Using a fluted pastry wheel, cut strips that measure 1 inch wide by 8 inches long. Gently tie the strips into bows. Pour the oil to a depth of 2 inches in a pot over medium flame and allow to heat up. Test the oil by dropping in a small pinch of dough; if the pinch sizzles and floats immediately, the oil is ready. Fry the bows in the hot oil, 2 or 3 at a time, until golden on all sides. Drain on paper towels, sprinkle with confectioners' sugar, and serve.

Makes about 18

Brutti Ma Buoni

Ugly but Good Cookies

What's in a name? In this case, everything. I defy anybody to find a better recipe title than this one. You can buy these delicious cookies at most Italian bakeries and pastry shops, and they are also easy to make at home. When I was a young kid, my grandmother would make these so I could leave them for Santa Claus on Christmas Eve. One Christmas I did a terrible thing. My grandmother had an antique nativity set that she had had for years. That year I noticed the baby Jesus had a dirty face. So I took a Brillo pad and scrubbed his face. But I scrubbed it so clean that I washed his eyes and mouth right off. I was horrified; I didn't know what to do. I asked my grandmother for extra Brutti Ma Buoni that year. "Why?" she asked. "I did something terrible," I explained. "If I give Santa some extra *brutti*, maybe he will think I'm *buoni*!"

1¼ pounds whole blanched almonds, lightly toasted

½ pound granulated sugar

6 extra-large egg whites

¼ teaspoon ground cinnamon

½ teaspoon vanilla extract

1 tablespoon unsalted butter, softened

1 tablespoon all-purpose flour

Finely chop ¾ pound of the nuts with 4 tablespoons of the sugar. Chop the next ¼ pound of nuts medium and the remaining ¼ pound coarsely. Mix all the nuts together.

Preheat the oven to 250°F.

Place the egg whites in a bowl. Use a wire whisk (make sure it's very clean) to whip the egg whites to a soft peak. Continue to beat as you add the remaining sugar a little at a time. Then add the nuts gradually. Add the cinnamon and the vanilla. Continue to mix, placing the bowl over medium heat for about 1 minute to dry out the mixture.

Lightly butter a baking sheet and dust it with the flour. Place 2 tablespoons–size mounds of the batter on the sheet about 1 inch apart. Bake in the oven for 45 minutes. Raise the temperature to 300°F. and bake for another 40 minutes. Remove the cookies from the sheet and allow to cool before serving.

Makes 26 cookies

Note: These cookies can be stored in an airtight container for up to 2 weeks.

Taralli

Lemon Cookies

In Naples, these tasty little nuggets are a traditional accompaniment to espresso. I did some digging around to find the best recipe and in the process I discovered quite a few variations and a number of different names. This version is sweet, but I also found some savory versions—with black pepper or even onion—that are meant to be served alongside a soup. In Naples they are called *taralli* or *frizelli*. I found a Sicilian version called *cuddureddi*. This one is my favorite, and I'm sure you'll love it, too.

For the dough
3½ cups all-purpose flour
½ teaspoon salt
2½ teaspoons baking powder
2½ teaspoons baking soda
6 tablespoons granulated sugar
Grated zest of 1 lemon
6 tablespoons unsalted butter, softened
1 cup milk
2 large eggs
2 teaspoons vanilla extract
Juice of 1 lemon

For the glaze
2 cups confectioners' sugar
Grated zest of ½ lemon
Juice of ½ lemon
2 tablespoons milk

Preheat the oven to 350°F.

TO PREPARE THE DOUGH: Combine the flour, salt, baking powder, baking soda, sugar, and lemon zest in a bowl. Make a well in the center and add the butter, milk, eggs, vanilla, and lemon juice. Mix by hand with a wooden spoon or for no more than 1 minute in an electric mixer until all the ingredients are incorporated and a sticky dough is formed.

Roll the dough, 1 tablespoon at a time, into ropes 10 inches long. Cut them in half, lay the halves side by side and intertwine them to form a twist. Form the twists into rings. Place a piece of parchment paper on a baking sheet and arrange the rings on it. Bake for 15 minutes or until lightly browned. Remove from the oven and allow to cool on the baking sheet.

TO PREPARE THE GLAZE: Combine all the ingredients and mix until smooth. Dip the top of each cookie into the glaze, then spread it evenly with your finger. Allow the glaze to dry at room temperature. Once the glaze is dry you can store the cookies in an airtight container for up to 2 weeks.

Makes 3 dozen

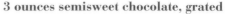

Fagottini di Mele

Apple Bundles

This is a recipe I recall fondly from my childhood. It originates with an old friend of the family named Antonetta, who came from a small town called Talese not far from Naples. Her husband, Tony, loved to make homemade wine. He loved drinking it even more. He would get drunk, start complaining about how poor they were, and eventually threaten to jump out the window. The only problem was they lived in the basement.

Amaretto di Saronno is the original almond-flavored liqueur from the town of Saronno outside of Milan. Now there are many imitators; sometimes it's made with almonds, other times with the kernels of apricot pits, which have a similar, pleasantly bitter flavor. Amaretti are the fantastic dry macaroon-type cookies made with a touch of the liqueur. It's a classic recipe, which you can find in my first book. You can also buy them in any Italian deli in tins under the Lazzaroni brand name.

3 ounces semisweet chocolate, grated

2 tablespoons unsalted butter, melted

5 amaretti (amaretto cookies), crumbled

3 tablespoons amaretto liqueur (preferably Amaretto di Saronno)

4 baking apples such as Golden Delicious or Rome

½ cup apricot jam, warmed

1 pound Puff Pastry Dough (page 196)

Flour for dusting

1 large egg, beaten

Preheat the oven to 450°F.

Thoroughly combine the chocolate, melted butter, amaretti, and amaretto in a mixing bowl.

Peel the apples then core them with a corer. Stuff the cored apples with the chocolate mixture, then brush them with the apricot jam.

Roll out the puff pastry dough to a thickness of ⅛ inch on a lightly floured surface. Cut out four rounds of dough large enough to cover the apples. Use the trimmings to cut out small leaves to decorate the pastries. Wrap each apple in a round of dough, sealing the base well. Brush the dough-covered apples with beaten egg, garnish with the pastry leaves, and place on a baking sheet at least 3 inches apart. Bake for 25 minutes or until golden brown. Serve warm.

Serves 4

Serving suggestion: These go great with your favorite ice cream.

Puff Pastry Dough

This recipe is a bit involved, calling for five repetitions of the folding, rolling, and chilling process, but that extra effort is rewarded with an exquisitely light, fluffy pastry.

2 cups unsalted butter

4 cups all-purpose flour

1 teaspoon salt

1 tablespoon lemon juice

Work the butter into a brick shape, 3 by 5 by 1½ inches.

Spoon 3 tablespoons of the flour onto a piece of parchment paper large enough to enclose the entire piece of butter. Use the parchment paper to coat the piece of butter with flour, then wrap the butter in the parchment paper and set aside.

Place the remaining flour in a large mixing bowl, make a well in the center, and add the salt, lemon juice, and 1 cup of water. Work the flour and water together, creating a firm but slightly sticky dough. Gradually add up to ⅓ cup more water if the dough seems to need the extra moisture. Knead the dough for about 15 minutes until it is very smooth and elastic. Form it into a ball, cover with a damp towel and allow to rest for 15 minutes.

Place the dough on a floured cloth (a clean dish towel works best), cut a cross or X shape in the center of the ball, cutting halfway to the bottom of the ball. Pull and roll out the four "ears" from the cross, leaving the center as a thick cushion. Place the brick of butter into the cushion. Stretch the four ears back over the butter, overlapping them and sealing the edges and corners. The dough should take on the rectangular shape of the butter. (*Note:* If the butter is too soft to hold its shape, chill it briefly in the fridge so it hardens up a bit before wrapping it in the dough.) After enclosing the butter in the dough, wrap the dough in the parchment paper again and chill in the fridge for 20 minutes.

On a floured cloth, roll out the dough as evenly as possible into a rectangle 8 by 18 inches and about ⅓ inch thick. Brush off the excess flour and fold the ends of the dough in as you would fold a business letter to put it into an envelope, forming a three-layered rectangle. Press the dough firmly. Fold the dough in half, pocketbook fashion, so that it has 6 layers. Wrap it in the parchment paper and chill for ½ hour in the fridge.

Place the dough on the floured cloth with the open end facing you. Roll the dough into a rectangle once more, the same size as it was originally, brush off the excess flour, and fold as before. Repeat the rolling and folding process 3 more times, chilling the dough for at least ½ hour after each time. Repeat the process one final time and then chill the dough for at least 3 hours at which point it is ready for use.

Makes 1 pound

Frappe

Crispy Carnival Pastries

These scrumptious pastries are a regular at celebrations in the Naples area. They are usually served just dusted with some confectioners' sugar. The fruit and sauce are a fancier touch.

For the pastries

1¾ cups all-purpose flour

3 large egg yolks

⅓ cup confectioners' sugar

½ teaspoon vanilla extract

Grated zest of 1 orange

1 tablespoon unsalted butter, melted

¼ teaspoon salt

1 tablespoon anisette liqueur

For the sauce

⅔ cup milk

½ cup heavy cream

3 large egg yolks

⅓ cup granulated sugar

½ teaspoon vanilla extract

1 tablespoon amaretto (preferably Amaretto di Saronno)

For the fruit

2 tablespoons unsalted butter

2 Golden Delicious apples, peeled, seeded, and cubed

2 medium-size pears, peeled, seeded, and diced

¼ cup granulated sugar

2 oranges, peeled and segmented

2 cups light neutral-tasting vegetable oil such as canola or safflower for frying

Confectioners' sugar for dusting

TO PREPARE THE PASTRIES: Mix the flour, egg yolks, confectioners' sugar, vanilla extract, orange zest, butter, salt, and anisette in a bowl until you have a smooth dough. Refrigerate for 1 hour.

After 1 hour, roll out the dough into sheets about ⅛ inch thick and cut them into 3-inch squares. Cut slits all the way through the sheets but not their full length. (Alternatively, use a lattice cutter or a pastry cutter.)

TO PREPARE THE SAUCE: Combine the milk and heavy cream in a saucepan over medium heat and bring to a boil. In a separate bowl, beat the egg yolks and the sugar together with a whisk. Whisk a ladleful of milk mixture into the egg yolks, then whisk the egg yolk mixture into the pan with the milk. Cook over medium-low heat for 3 to 4 minutes or until thick enough to lightly coat the back of a spoon. Whisk in the vanilla and amaretto; cool.

Preheat the oven to 450°F.

TO PREPARE THE FRUIT: Heat the butter in an ovenproof skillet, then add the apples and pears. Place the skillet in the oven and bake for 5 minutes or until lightly browned. Sprinkle with the sugar and the oranges and cook for another 8 minutes or until caramelized.

Place the oil in a heavy-bottomed pot to a depth of 3 inches and heat to 350°F over a medium-high flame. Test the oil by dropping in a small piece of batter. When it floats and sizzles immediately, the oil is ready for frying. Fry the pastries in the oil until golden brown and crispy on both sides. Drain on paper towel; dust with confectioners' sugar. Ladle sauce onto each plate, then spoon a mound of fruit into the middle of each. Position the warm pastries on the fruit.

Serves 6

Torta di Amaretto

Amaretto Cake

I've been friends with Vito Bari for a long time. In fact, you could say we've been friends since *before* we were born, because his family is from Naples and they were friends with my relatives over there before anybody came to America. As is often the case in Italy, the Baris' lives revolved around the Catholic Church. In that tradition, Friday is confession day. I remember when we were kids, Vito was so terrified to go into the confessional booth that when it came time to tell the priest his sins he would never say anything. He couldn't remember them. Finally his mother had him write them down. After Vito left the booth, his mother checked with the priest: Again, no sins. . . . "Vito, what happened?" his mother asked. "Were you too scared to read your sins?" "No, Mama," Vito replied. "It was too dark in there!"

By the way, this terrific recipe comes from Vito's late mother.

7 ounces white chocolate

One 8-inch sponge cake

½ cup amaretto liqueur (preferably Amaretto di Saronno)

24 amaretti (amaretto cookies)

1 recipe Pastry Cream (page 218)

1⅔ cups heavy cream, whipped

Break the chocolate into pieces and melt in a double boiler. Remove from the heat. Cut a strip of parchment paper 3 inches wide and long enough to wrap around the sponge cake. Brush one side of the paper with the warm chocolate.

Brush the sponge cake liberally with ¼ cup of the amaretto liqueur, then wrap it with the strip of parchment paper, the chocolate on the inside. Press gently so the chocolate adheres to the cake. Place in a freezer until the chocolate hardens, then peel off the paper.

Crumble all but 9 amaretto cookies into the pastry cream, add the remaining liqueur, then fold in gently three quarters of the whipped cream. Spread the cream mixture onto the cake, smoothing the top. Using a pastry bag, pipe out 9 rosettes—or whatever other decoration you like—of the whipped cream on top of the cake, garnishing each one with a cookie. (Alternatively, use a spoon.) Refrigerate for at least 1 hour before serving.

Serves 10

Taralluci Dolci

Sweet Taralluci

These ring-shaped biscuits are a typical Neapolitan treat. They're so popular that there is an expression, *a taralluci e vino*, which means "there will be a happy ending," and in fact they're often accompanied with wine—either a sweet dessert wine such as *vin santo* or just a good glass of red. So take the afternoon off, settle into an armchair out on the porch, and enjoy a glass of wine and a plate of taralluci.

> **3 medium eggs, plus 1 beaten egg**
>
> **⅔ cup granulated sugar, mixed with ¼ teaspoon vanilla extract**
>
> **3 tablespoons anisette liqueur**
>
> **1 teaspoon ground cinnamon**
>
> **¾ teaspoon anise seed**
>
> **3 cups all-purpose flour**
>
> **Vegetable oil for frying**

Beat the 3 eggs in a bowl with the sugar. Add the anisette, cinnamon, and anise seed and beat with a whisk until all ingredients are well incorporated. Add the flour and continue to mix all the ingredients in the bowl until you have a smooth dough. Cover the bowl with a damp cloth and refrigerate for 1 hour.

On a lightly floured surface, roll pieces of the dough about the size of a plum into sausage shapes about 6 inches long and ½ inch thick. Form each sausage shape into a ring by crossing the ends over and pressing them together. Seal the ends with a little beaten egg.

Place vegetable oil in a pot over medium heat to a depth of 2 inches. Test the oil by dropping in a small piece of batter; if it floats and sizzles right away, the oil is ready. Fry the rings 2 or 3 at a time. After 30 seconds, remove the rings and make an incision along the top so they will split open when you return them to the oil. Fry them until golden brown, about 3 minutes total. Drain on paper towels, allow to cool, and serve.

Makes about 30 biscuits

Torta di Nocciole

Hazelnut Cake

Most of the recipes for *torta* that I've come across are for savory tarts or pies rather than the sweet dessert ones. Here is a wonderful exception, a cake that is easy to bake at home and incredibly delicious, offering the smooth richness of ricotta and the intoxicating flavor of lightly roasted hazelnuts.

4½ ounces hazelnuts

4 ounces unsalted butter, softened

½ cup granulated sugar, plus 2 tablespoons

4 large eggs, separated

3½ tablespoons all-purpose flour, sifted

4½ ounces ricotta cheese

2 teaspoons grated lemon zest

**6 tablespoons apricot jam, mixed with
    1 tablespoon water**

1 ounce semisweet chocolate, finely grated

Preheat the oven to 375°F.

Place the hazelnuts on a baking sheet and bake them in the oven for 10 minutes or until golden brown. Allow the nuts to cool, rub off their skins, and finely chop them.

Place the butter in a mixing bowl and beat it together with the ½ cup of sugar. Add the egg yolks and continue to beat until light and fluffy, about 3 minutes, then fold in the flour.

In a separate bowl, beat the ricotta cheese until it's a smooth consistency, then add the chopped nuts and lemon zest. Add this mixture to the flour-egg yolk mixture. Beat the egg whites till you have stiff peaks, beat in the remaining 2 tablespoons of sugar, and fold this mixture into the ricotta mixture.

Butter a 10-inch tart pan, place the mixture in the pan, spread it around evenly, and bake in the oven for ½ hour. Remove the pan from the oven, allow the tart to cool, then turn it over and remove the pan. Spread the jam evenly over the top of the tart, sprinkle with the grated chocolate, allow to cool to room temperature, and serve.

Serves 8

Torrone di Noce

Walnut Brittle

When I was a kid, *torrone* was the treat of treats. I'd resort to almost anything to get my hands on a piece of it. Torrone can be eaten as is, or crushed as a topping for cakes or as a layer for a homemade ice cream cake. Be careful, though; it's also addictive.

Vegetable oil
½ cup granulated sugar
½ cup honey
3 tablespoons freshly squeezed orange juice
2 cups walnut pieces

Lightly grease a baking sheet with vegetable oil. Combine the sugar, honey, and orange juice in a saucepan over low heat. When the sugar is melted, add the walnuts. Cook for 3 to 4 minutes or until golden and thick. Pour onto the oiled sheet and spread it out to cool. While the brittle is still hot, use a large knife to score the mixture into 2-inch pieces. When the brittle is cool, break the pieces where you had scored them. Store airtight.

Makes 1½ cups brittle